murphy formally bound

triplets

001 the confabulation of details
002 the written word freezes the voice
003 i do my puzzles, most times in ink
004 i tell my story whole, between the fits and starts of life
005 poetry is mere ego rampant
006 attention now is the past remembered
007 i will not in grey hours revoke
008 i continue to stuff the crevices of memory
009 hard smooth milky white
010 it was one of those times of near strength
011 i told it all to her, she listened
012 my death songs, telling what-i-remembers
013 nobody expects the retard
014 the chill of christmas penetrates
015 there's a cardinal down a few trees from me
016 'tis but a pittance that i feel
017 there's brunch, then tea, then a supper
018 we wrestle with the lessons of our time
019 the thickness of liquidity makes mud
020 the examined life, thinking it through
021 i remember when i worked in business
022 i remember walking down into the back pastures
023 i have some time these days
024 i am no devotee of the endgame
025 asked one time about the sanctity of life
026 backward psychology
027 a slow garden morning in the chill of early spring
028 the clamor of ignorance forges a hammer of hatred
029 i wonder if the middle of the stream
030 wisdom takes practice
031 (wisdom takes practice)
032 that's the accuracy
033 insects are banished from my sheltered cave

quintets

035 my god is dead. he died one day
036 sense rarely comes the way
037 that's the accuracy
038 the fluidity of the tumbling blood
039 i am a creature of my place
040 it's interesting to see it all from this end
041 you have to understand about words
042 five thousand steps one at a time
043 the way harmony travels

couplets

045 i'm not sorry i haven't solved the three body problem
046 i walk a hidden path he said
047 i feel the sag of water's flow
048 an eremite i have become
049 if you are the spring sower of seed
050 i saw an ant hill stomped the other day
051 outside my windows it rains with a steady pace
052 i taste the world as concrete dust

two quatrains

054 you have left me here alone and i am hurting
055 when a man is fully aware of all living creatures
056 this winter seems to come too soon
057 the ferocity of a moment is rarely achieved
058 three weeks later i started to cry
059 there are no right angles in nature
060 the mad lady of my mind will squabble now
061 sometimes i watch netflix for the news
062 my hand wet and cold, i hold an icy drink
063 i was asked to sweep the floor, look busy
064 i herd my wily cats, those stealthy thoughts
065 a restless wind in these first few days of april

066 ransom notes can pinpoint worth
067 memory wriggles the brain of my oak floor
068 i sit at the edge of a storm
069 my ship has docked, the luggage cleared
070 the swooping bird, the mocking bird

three quatrains

072 old men of power lose their edge, their nose
073 i remember listening to a special one
074 i no longer swim into an ocean of future
075 sore moves this winter down
076 so i just had my whiskey breakfast
077 the dime of death short stops us all
078 words have a putative power
079 fuzzywhumps and fizzigigs
080 we were herded together at harvard
081 translation is misunderstood
082 there is a difference
083 scales fall from rheumy eyes of evening
084 old things come back, unbidden, whole
085 my mind is trained, it seeks the why
086 it's a stately sail in this soft breeze
087 i've come to the time of departure
088 i, I, and eye agree
089 i have now to decide, maintenance or joy
090 fug of tobacco tastes the room
091 dull red the brick of my back-yard wall
092 afloat on the calm baltic sea
093 this night will open softly for my thrust
094 rain stains the silver of my soul
095 totality of view slowly fills in
096 the sacred heart of all i am
097 the bridge goes up in fog
098 shifting grey is oblique sky
099 a circle runs within my mind
100 late summer green glistens

101 i've found a cave to hide within
102 i slippery, eelily, watch all my spielery
103 faint glow of misty lights suffuse through glass
104 did i tell you today that i love you
105 beauty must have a place that shows
106 a faux pas is chaos of water
107 two things at once seems normal

four quatrains

109 how imagine an ancestor you've never known
110 (how imagine an ancestor you've never known)
111 salty slush of urban snow
112 the focusing on markovian connections
113 i reorganize the world in the mornings
114 mist wet of cold is wind
115 i wonder why the ending starts so soon
116 a terrible wetness of late afternoon
117 the heat is pregnant, its music sultry
118 i thought that once was all i had
119 my cave has light these lately evenings
120 dark morning sky is thick with cloud
121 a sharp shattering sleet on my face
122 slanted shadow flickers through bus window
123 a wholesome heart weathers the rain
124 a woven warp of dimness lies across my bed this night
125 beware the poet in his cups
126 quiddity jibbety, then equanimity
127 the pen i wield captures me
128 the sound it is which thrills as thought
129 water pools despite one's caring
130 early light, mist rising, down to water's edge
131 dull color of sleet is my face
132 there's a peculiar problem in man's most
133 i looked around and knew at once
134 the cardinal swooped down into the yard
135 the summer seems indian in its soft intent

136 a baboon circling the meadows
137 do little i know anything
138 i am but a man, and i have two feet
139 i became a river of voices
140 i came home to the clean house
141 i fly above the cares of the world
142 i hear a crickle in the fluorescent lights
143 i know the circles of heaven
144 i learned enough to gather food
145 i still cook the careful meals
146 is my practice now my purpose
147 legs become more leaden than not
148 my father told me about memory
149 sadness bursts through the dunes
150 my ultimate god like my ultimate father
151 now let's see how inky the streak
152 roiling clouds bedaub with grey
153 the thing is, how hard do you push others away
154 to me fear of death is always in the doing
155 trickster is medicine
156 try to carve out a place for your self
157 words, the twisting maze of chosen way
158 you carry the world with you
159 a rolling thunder comes my way
160 i guess i turned out to be what i wanted
161 an orange cast to the bricks across the way

five and more quatrains

163 i nod in ease and know i'll sleep
164 a cooling breeze and clear bright day
165 a spitting rain and fretful wind
166 a wholesome tongue labors to say the truth
167 my daughter asked today when i will die
168 so what is rest for a marmot
169 the thought is difficult to entrain
170 a child i was when old age began

171 earth is testing me these days
172 i found these old writings in a book
173 i was watching television in the ninth grade
174 memory is a fragile sense in modern times
175 moccasins report concrete, unyielding
176 my first granddaughter is pugnacious
177 i want a primeval nose
178 when i was a young man, an indian in the city
179 the words came flat and cold, unbidden
180 i mention to you this morning the sadness i feel
181 the slow grey morning sits outside
182 the rexographs and pentiums

asian forms

taalagi 7 line

185 poetic forms are battlefields
186 i got a buffalo nickel in my change today
187 i climbed the mountain of my life and am almost back
down
188 a wise woman taught me the craft of weaving
189 sometimes i go the long way around
190 thoughts aren't thoughts until they're worded
191 water seeps into the ground
192 little one who asks to come to wisdom
193 for a while when i was young i prospered
194 we are going to the orchard to sing, don't forget your guitar
195 i am the firekeeper who kindles the fire of truth
196 strip bare your heart, throw its clothes in the ditch
197 i can never know the truth of the earth's creation
198 i lost all my odes and love poems to the water
199 the spirit which placed fire in my spirit
200 i dance a waltz through the rooms of night
201 the spirit gives me the joy and splendor i crave

sijo

(not) knowing the answer (6 poems)

203 wait in fear   wait in silence
204 choose each time   to be a moment
205 anger red   start and startle
206 seven stars   shine from nowhere
207 mist of morning   hot, dark coffee
208 sit and wait   as a mountain

more sijo

209 damp gusty cold   this march of wind
210 autumn sky   puffs cold magic
211 blue sky hidden   phantom sky
212 cool wind gusting   whipping tree
213 don't bother with   a straw mat
214 eastern sun   fade westerly
215 greying drops   of stained concrete
216 late spring day   steal first feeling
217 look outside   cold clear window
218 pound on pound   goes my fist down
219 settle down   water run pool
220 squeaking snow   beneath my feet
221 summer green   yet a dreaming
222 sun so pure   startle color
223 wander more   feet reluctant
224 war is come   dig through rubble
225 it's all there   each stab at perfection

murphy shih

227 bright   cool   wind   fresh   morning
228 cold   sweep   bend   trees   limbs
229 early   blossom   heart   stop   beauty
230 steam   hiss   bang   heat   rise

231 bramble   creek   tumble   stone   roll
232 man   leisure   apple   blossom   evening

haiku

a rubaiyat

242 i am a lazy
   look down the wind that always comes
243 early morning arousal is immoderate
   it's only a matter of integrity
244 i eat ice cream
   the mind's differential
245 to check a building
   purity is a wasted emotion
246 the ground is quiet, dormant.
   my love is like a nice cool night
247 the thin leafed trees are full with wind
   i don't argue with my rhythm's surge
248 the magic carpet does not tempt my feet
   there is no music for the dance this special night
249 when you sing your body tunes in habit
   i like it best when we don't talk
250 my animal lair is dense with my smell
   my muse bustles around her piano bench
251 what's a library for if not to read
   i don't eat like a lark
252 dive to the bottom of your river
   i learned long ago that the river knows
253 it's a cruel sad day in amarillo
   bend the future by remembering the past
254 chappaqua, chippewa, who gives a shit
   i crowed to the sun when he appeared this morning
255 i dig through piles and piles of thoughts
   i got a brand new body just last week

256 i idle along my personal river
   i know my enemy when i hold him in my hands
257 i love the mixing water of estuary
   i need not know how hard it is
258 i practice my music in the whole of its form
   i read a lot when i buy the books
259 i sit in the shade of a bank near ripples
   i started as a boulder tumbling off the cliff
260 i stretch the limousine which is my heart
   i wander the keys of my life's piano
261 it's a matter of integrity
   i've tossed my bait out into the pond
262 my backwardness becomes full forward
   my dampened dawn is grey with mist
263 my daughters are sharing their first born child
   my ganglions have grown dull these last few years
264 my melody invites when out of tune
   my smell is concordant with fear
265 my thoughts are creeks in their downward flow
   one should understand the balance of things
266 the artist still knows why practice is all
   the grass by my front door is dead and gone
267 the greens fresh picked are dark in leaf
   the kitchen i cook in has a warm, used look
268 why are my thoughts always an ocean
   why are you listening to all my ravings
269 you yowl like a cat that feels the heat
   sore comes the winter down
270 when a circle becomes a community

triplets

the confabulation of details
in written words, which often sing
the thereness of the feelings brought along

the conturbation of mind's eye
to hear the words leap off the page
their melodies the inner dance of time

murphy reading shakespeare in bed

the written word freezes the voice
to wait, to melt in other mental worlds
in other times, to melt into meaning

the spoken word raises the voice
to action, to stir the winds in others
in that heard time, to rouse into feeling

the singing word chords the voice
to splendor, to burrow body deep in others
in that felt time, to ring, tingling within

murphy burnishing his craftiness

i do my puzzles, most times in ink
the simple numbers, the interlaced words
the sounds of patterns, the readings of books

i work with my hands, sometimes in dirt
the artistic tools, the painted works of art
the sculpted solidities, the music of instrument

i work with my heart, sometimes i hurt
the outreach of hands, the warmth of the hug
the natural of kissing, the doing of love

murphy waiting for gravity to take hold

i tell my story whole, between the fits and starts of life
small snippets, stitched together in a welter mode
the upset of discovery when chance reveals the code

the blur of movement stolen in a moment's song
the piles of thought upheavals, the achings of the heart
the slow grind of betterment, habit become an art

wordy voice of wisdom woven strong
the sake' worth the sip of attention
in the joyful easy float of play

murphy reducing thought to the page

poetry is mere ego rampant
the all seeing eye, the singing ear
so why not the i of me i hear

or remember in the telling scene
an exactness bringing back the whole
i admit i stage it all, i screen

arrange the deck for dealings done
prescribe the way we all are one
so i affirm, each genetic bit of me

murphy bellying up to the bar

attention now is the past remembered
intrusive in the perfection of its song
ringing mind's thickest bell of thought

attention then is happenstance recalled
incisive in its pulling up the file
from deep within the chaos of the pile

attention new is the wish for what may be
corrosive as life's etching of a skin
on what is now the when of all that's been

murphy packed and ready to go

i will not in grey hours revoke
the gift i give in hours of light
before the breath of slander broke
the thread of folly drew me tight

a frizzled thread weak hope had made
to bind two lonely hearts as one
but lights of love will fade and fade
while all the moods of men are spun

the gift i gave once more i give
for you when comes the winter time
for you white flower of beauty live
at edge of pool in liquid rhyme

i continue to stuff the crevices of memory
untidily cramming the new with the old
deep into the ravine of stored wonder

i continue to imagine the haloes of future
the glowing circles of what yet may be
spreading to fill the sky with their nimbi

i continue to rise to the light of new morning
glory being tempered with the creaks of old age
weathered visage accepting whatever may come

mlk

hard smooth milky white
marble crypt placed in bright
crowded sunshine

pungent blooms of varied hue
placed on high as if his view
were yours and mine

next day mist and bone
smell of earth, smell of stone
bouquet of wine

it was one of those times of near strength
when i thought to myself of the worth
of standing beside my own hearth

i was reminded of ancient man
bending to his forge
fashioning fendable edges

not of the modern sort of softness
of men stacked midst stainless swords
of swaddling missile steel

i told it all to her, she listened
i listened and she finally told
it was nice after that for us both

i strutted for her as she watched
25 books, four or five songs
acrostic poetry, i poured it on

she understood it all, asked shyly for more
i danced through our days, she dancing along
i walk slower now, a meandering way

my death songs, telling what-i-remembers
sitting here in my comfy chair, feet on desk
staring out the window at the world astir

they're guaranteed to be burnished
as the brushing cloth of time smooths
and simplifies, as water does

the thrall of emotion, depicted, obliquely
sliding out either side of lines sung
the everchanging image in my mind

nobody expects the retard
the dodo, the stumbling ape
nobody expects the patience

it takes a long time to evolve
to acquire the nested intricacies
the orchestra, to make music

nobody looks at a turtle's slog
the careful, protected, gentle lurch
nobody expects endurance

the chill of christmas penetrates
the time of cold begins its linger
i rummage through old scribbled notes

the flowers i sang to mark our days
the mounting pile i prune and sort
arrange the moments as complements

recurrent themes, the special occasions
the everydayness of how it was
each inky streak a full mind's picture

there's a cardinal down a few trees from me
down to the left out the back window
beyond my craning sight

he sings the song i know of
down below my thoughts of care
far beyond what i recall

the red bird sings in crowning
top feathers spread, unfurled
tossed in their maleness, flaunted

'tis but a pittance that i feel
this long grey afternoon
this my last best time of all

'tis but a sufferance of my wounds
dull ache behind the grinning thought
these last thick clots of what it means

'tis but a prolonged grace of saying
the dance begun is song begun
the lilting gait that opens always

'tis but a pittance that i fill
each moment of my being
the craggy mountain of their pile

there's brunch, then tea, then a supper
til dawn, then lunch, then a dinner
the time is the thing

there's break, then work, then you go home
to roost, food and drink, then the tv
sublime as the king

there's scotch, then gin, then a kuyper
to launch, then smash, then the small talk
the rhyme makes it sing

there's red, then white, then a sake'
to freeze, then ease, then the snuggle
a dime buys a fling

we wrestle with the lessons of our time
roustabout texan to gentleman scholar
one's background tells

we settle for a vision when we learn
timid schoolboy to wry savant
one' s thinking grows

we nestle for a common sense of warmth
horny teenager to wrinkled old guy
one's hunger lasts

we fasten on image in the mirror
fashion mamas to dowager's flash
one's ego sings

the thickness of liquidity makes mud
and rain these last three days of wet
thr slickened sheen of greasy water drowns

no constant hold against the downward flow
will tell, will hold the very fundament in hold
the slither swift as ease of long held breath

and gasp of new is lunging grasp of being
where sun will often dry the leaves of time
the flicks of form within the thought of go

i wallow when the words wall high with meaning
i note the cling of feelings when they're here
they flicker on my inmost movie screen

the examined life, thinking it through
love of self enough to do it the best
attention paid, always, and remembered

the coagulation into clots of certainty
satisfactions of doubt, ink pens of flourish
behind, between, beside, betwixt the flow

for it seems all is movement in an ocean gale
no direction but wind that will erratic blow
that's real, that blusters the push of change

that makes the path more wide and steady
inevitable if chosen in hindsight wisdom
a satisfaction of effort when retold to the young

i remember when i worked in business
folding cartons the products we sold
and i dressed fine enough to pass

i remember how ephemeral the goals
next week, tomorrow, the end of the month
we were salesmen who guaranteed orders

i remember learning new voices, new ways
each pitch to make i made a listen to learn
and i was good in finding new business

i remember when it all went away
the reason for the hustle, the why of it all
and i was free to seek my own path

i remember walking down into the back pastures
my grandfather's farm, where he ended up, in texas
we were going to replace the salt lick for the animals

his small stock of cattle were the main lickers
though all the other animals who could reach it
they all licked there too, and so should you, he said

it was a strange tasting salt, richer in flavors, sea like
if i had but known what the sea tasted like
back there, landlocked in deep north east texas

we all need salt, the old man said, every animal
and you, my son, are only the desendent of animals
watch their habits, they teach what you should know

i have some time these days
i can herd my turtles of thought
those that have stuck to me all these years

they run as deep and as slow as loggerheads
as slashing as red eared sliders
but always in and around water

no terrapins have i on my bank
no dry slogs through desert earth of heat
no ponderous plodding gait to there

just captured moments in their flesh
all the directions clearly seen
a swimming tank of dreams

i am no devotee of the endgame
bloom of seed much more my style
yet here i sit, enchaired, remembering

the smallest bit adds to the sum of it all
i glean vagaries of the past with my mind
i smile, i gaze beyond, i reason what is left

the aches beside, the crumbling teeth
the stiffness of morning, the tiredness of night
sip the booze, enjoy, lean back, appraise

now the ending, ice come to changing form
all the pulsing, all my body's living cells
all the books, the words, the thoughtful songs

asked one time about the sanctity of life
the wise man said take sanctity to wife
then find your peace

asked one time about the shortness of life
the aged man said take today as your goal
then find your way

asked one time about the reason for life
the crafty man said it's all that you are
then you are gone

asked one time about the life of reason
the wary man said it at least points a way
then you attend

backward psychology
is seeing an urban crazy woman
and learning her craziness

as psychotherapy, for the empath
must visit madness to understand
the sane

as developmental understanding
of urban indian proficient protagonist
with constant thoughts about medicine

and the place one must find in the world
the world one has inherited
the one-way complexity to the end

a slow garden morning in the chill of early spring
a youngster's peal of laughter in his tipsy first few steps
the lesson so gradually learned of circle's rhythm

steamy late afternoon in the full heat of summer
a young man as athlete, a warrior giving us his all
birth and death, water's downward path

the pungence of fall's bounty beginning the end of it all
a full grown man of substance, responsible to self alone
the slow senescence of a decaying remnant

the pull of wintry pain freezing life on earth
an old man's special, patient place, in recurrence of time
the grandeur of having lived, awake to it all

the clamor of ignorance forges a hammer of hatred
drowns considered wisdom, the reflection of water
pooling to clarity, creating unique depth of vision

the callous, selfish disregard, the wealthy privilege
infects with the waking dreams of fearful others
builds protective walls, withstands imagined siege

each man, woman, and child is an entitlement
to a life, safety, comfort, and liberty assumed
fault the education system which has failed its mission

a democracy that works, that brings the most prosperity to all
that brings the progress of knowledge gained and used
is built on the collective voice of considered civic reason

we have failed to arm the people with this strength of mind
so it is understood by all, that the gift of life is treasured
so each and every one of us has fair chance at happiness

i wonder if the middle of the stream
gives the proper downhill slide to dream
the rhythm of the richness of the ride

i stagger down the middle of the street
quite vainly hope my strides are neat
enough to get me back to where i hide

i seldom catch the volume of my thought
til it is over, snaggled tight, and caught
copy-cat that notates talk sits by my side

i often find myself in the middle of these days
staring obliquely at the sun, its sparkling rays
a verdant trap that i allow to grow inside

i float as leaf within the belly of my rhyme
that flashes up to videos of time
that cut apart the wholeness of those who've died

wisdom takes practice
wisdom takes time
wisdom takes a leap

it must be made habit
it must be dwelt upon
it must be a novelty

automatic, unthought
for a moment and for ever
for the jaded, for the quick

a distillation of breaths
a recollection of thoughts
the close cut fingernail

a fermentation under control
a congery made to order
the stabbing hold on life

wisdom takes practice
it must be made habit
automatic, unthought
a distillation of breaths
a fermentation under control

wisdom takes time
it must be dwelt upon
for a moment and for ever
a recollection of thoughts
a congery made to order

wisdom takes a leap
it must be a novelty
for the jaded, for the quick
the close cut fingernail
the stabbing hold on life

wisdom takes practice
wisdom takes time
wisdom takes a leap

that's the accuracy
the particularity of event
that leads before this fragile face

the perspicacity of events
that led to this last easiness of days
the swarming slaver of their feast

that led to this warm softness of place
this endless ocean we slowly crawl
that glints in eye

this warm ingle snug from winter's place
the storms betimes
that's the acumen of taut old age

those crowds outside
that's the audacity
the persistency of event

insects are banished from my sheltered cave
screens on the windows, seals on the floors
poisons target the intrepid intruders

my roof doesn't leak, my doors all have locks
the fire glows inside when i turn on the gas
the ice box electric, and cools all the time

the water runs hot, the water runs cold
tame ions do chores without my control
i let it all happen and imagine i'm home

the earth is our mother and messily feeds us
and she whips us with storms and with floods
when angry she wrinkles her crust, tears buildings down

we came from her womb along with all her insects
we shut ourselves off from their world and we lose
no more should we hope to keep out the germs

all those small lives we battle, they change as we fight them
all those large lives we end, we force their extinction
all those dreams that we have, we lose in the morning

a globe has no sealant, it rounds out its welcome
a direction to center is all that it takes
a determined trajectory aimed at its target

so why build up walls, why not open our systems
survive as we must by accepting complexity
there is no way to live if you screen out the bugs

quintets

my god is dead. he died one day
i remember when it was
he died so hard the sun's first ray
was seen as though through gauze
but seen it was

my mind's alive. i see the sun
i feel just what it does
this is my work and just begun
it's seen as though through gauze
it's what one does

    cp

sense rarely comes the way
we tell our clotured lives
the shams we show today
snicker through as knives
yammering inside our heads

there should be times we're free
from fears of failing scenes
a subtle reality
become an end of means
a successful might-have-said

our thoughts would prey their way
from toe to tongue to them
the elusive sense of may
at once the cold hard gem
of once and twice through read

cp

that's the accuracy
the perspicacity of events
that led to this warm softness of place
this warm ingle snug from winter's face
those crowds outside

that's the audacity
the particularity of event
that led to this last easiness of days
this endless ocean we slowly crawl
the storms betimes

that's the acumen of taut old age
the persistency of event
that leads before this fragile face
the swarming slaver of their feast
that glints in eye

the fluidity of the tumbling blood
the river's roisterous rumbling flow
the electrons glow, attract, repulse
in broadcast of solid crumbling forms
radiating their cling, their distancing

complex interlocking animalcules
complex cascades of the pulsation of form
the building blocks maintaining their role
this minuscule world of warfare and death
this swirl of activity which is life

the swirl of activity which is life
the minuscule world of warfare and death
the building blocks maintaining the whole
complex cascades of pulsating forms
complex interlocking molecules

radiating their cling, their distancing
in broadcast of solid tumbling forms
the electrons glow, attract, repulse
in river's boisterous jumbling flow
the fluidity of the tumbling blood

i am a creature of my place
the frame of window i look outside
i tend to sit with right hand out
toward the feral, right outside
my careful protectment

i am a creature of my mind
the plastic lens i bend and swirl
i tend to watch my ears see dance
to recognize then realize
the flower in the phrase

i am a creature of my voice
the giveaway to what i feel
i tend to telegraph my thought
so all is nods then glance aside
the freshness of approach

i am a creature of my hands
that hold quite tight asleep at night
i tend to be obsessive
in making sure we're all alive
this day we have this morning

it's interesting to see it all from this end
the full stretch-of-arc-coming-to-ground end
the gentle humor in the irony of it all
those many wasted opportunities
those truly transcendant moments

it is interesting to finally be in that place
where pull of gravity meets with growing pain
the sheer miracle of how long i've lasted
the chaotic pile of books i've read
the food, the people, those who have touched me

it's interesting to reach into that convolution of mind
finely tempered with the ammunition of experience
to final understandings found in memories
glow of pride in good ones, the princely pile of wincing pain
the ultimate inadequacy of my errant efforts

you have to understand about words
they can be used in different patterns
developed exact meanings strung together
bursts of melody shrouded in chords
they have the power to change us

some of us talk the lingo, some of us sing
it's in the words, their colors, their magic
your imagination and the feelings it brings
the inner movie of dreams brought with the words
the fullness needed of their using, their sting

five thousand steps one at a time
with careful tread on yielding ground
soft skin molding foot to clutch of earth
to follow the river and learn its ways
from mountains pitch to soft ess curl

float downstream round bend on bend
lose trail of back in rambling course
splash through rapids scraping skin
to find the sea of what has been
since new born thought came clear

wind and tide harsh in crashing waves
the salt accepting water slosh
the breathing deep as water breathes
to find the place of balance
last pulsing push of gravity

the way harmony travels
reveals self in polity
lets one see the sum of yous
that you have shown
in growing free to choose

it's something easier
to sit at home and poke the fire
and pin the self to sense of self
flaring fair as sweet eye's choir
as melting sea as muse

will tend her fire of using me
to see the whole in bookish charm
in fiction remembered as history
and spoken fresh each leaving storm
of inky me come loose

couplets

i'm not sorry i haven't solved the three body problem
i'm forgiving myself for not learning more about love

    i drink a bit in my shallow afternoons
    and wake the side of brain that's cold

i'm not driven now by my imagined epic poems
i've rid myself of desire for wanton rhyme

    i chop my food for those i will be feeding
    and wake the side of brain that's bold

i'm not feeling bad for those girls who flirt their feelings
i'm freshened now and love a single, close

    i pick up pen to scrawl a crawling message
    and wake the side of brain that molds

i'm not certain here exactly what i'm doing
i've lost the frame and gained the flow of ease

    i gaze outside to manage nature's calling
    and wake the side of brain that holds

to only life i have as now unfolds

i walk a hidden path he said
my feet know not the way

i swim a winding stream he said
the way is no straight street

i dig a filling hole he said
my life is what i give

i build a sturdy wall he said
the gift is how i live

i train for an olympics
and wonder how i'll do

i feel the sag of water's flow
down, always down, to settle pond

i see the sag in withered plants
surest sign of the winter beyond

i know the shortness of my new time
that opens arms to welcome me

i am this kettle's turn to steam
i catch it now to halt the scream

an eremite i have become
a cave dweller who watches the climate

a stalagmite of ground emergent
a loneliness of process done

a safety, a protected sleeping
a quietude inside, a focus

a sparkling of atoms within the night
an evenness of inner sight

if you are the spring sower of seed
i am a tornado of destruction

if you are the lakota dog soldier
i am a cherokee scribe

if you are the chic parisienne
i am a plump loaisida

if you are the japanese sushi chef
i am a korean garlic head

if you are the sure footed sherpa
i am a mud mucking miner

if you are the suave manhattanite
i am a hooch swilling redneck

if you are end of the party
i am an onset of scarlet fever

i saw an ant hill stomped the other day
i watched the critters run away

they ran around, and then aground
ran all over to their sacred mound

the place they were and the way they lived
their practiced social niceties

the smells of rank, their fast ordering
the useful castes kept true, distinct

until other force came stomping round
to smash the world of all their ground

those small others way off down there
beneath the feet of those that own

who walk the earth with clumsy stride
where oh where can the ants go hide

outside my windows it rains with a steady pace
in this cool sweet, wet sweet, blossomy summer

inside my rooms the steady hum of thought
tossed carefully outward to meet with water's grace

i seed my dreams thus free to be in time
to start their life without me as further source

thought dream caught unfolding in elegance of rhyme
a cat's purr insistent, soft in inward ear

they burn in you as always in dreaming time and space
where best chance is seized upon with dancing hand

to let a thin wood pencil communicate my mind
my sense of nature's beauty, uniqueness formed with grace

i taste the world as concrete dust
my lungs by smog despoiled

i see the scars we all inflict
in carving up the space

i hear a constant motor hum
besmirched by siren's wail

i wonder why my inner voice
thinks words will catch the truth

i feel with lips, arthritic hands
that hurt their tender touching

i sense the all-around crash through
and burst the ego's dancing

two quatrains

you have left me here alone and i am hurting
stop this nonsense now, come back and hold me
stay beside me so eyes can swallow your face
that look, that time, that last warm you

stop your leaving, reach back home to touch
come back here to show your sad warm eyes
i ache, my arms, to hold the past as time
my heart in hand, to see your face at last

when a man is fully aware of all living creatures
he lives, his life as true as nature
as the happiest fish in the deepest pool
as the fully leafed tree inviting all birds

an old man accepts his fate, frail or sick
it wouldn't be better were he rich or important
the bones get up to walk in cold weather
the mouth tastes, chews the coarse meal of morning

this winter seems to come too soon
before our fall has started
grey frosty breaths depict
the ice of speech we're near

near enough, i'm sure
to wrap us in cocoons
of trusting, timeful faith
in thawing to difference

the ferocity of a moment is rarely achieved
by such foggy minded human animals as we are
it is terminally elusive to find such a total focus
i used to do it though, on the field of battle, play battle

i tore myself up waging war on football fields
fake war, but war that comes with all its scarrings
that learns the pain of death and then more living
to limp along a maundering path at times, that moment

three weeks later i started to cry
let myself go to the feelings i held
deep inside, hidden, neglected
three weeks later i started to cry

remembering the first loss so long, long ago
the tears then streamed, a young man's tears
now they just seep their old slow salty way
three weeks later i started to cry

there are no right angles in nature
unless freakish and different in form
from the fractals of life space emerging
the writhe of reach transformed by sun

bringing frills of twigging and leafing
balancing the chaos with the lifting beneath
sending roots with a steadfast of twisting
sending the rise above to shadeless space

the mad lady of my mind will squabble now
with all i know and love, with all i hear
she shouts a curse that's for me alone
in her need for primacy of chord

she takes a music and spits it out
she complexifies the joy
she never flows life's melodies
mad lady as she takes her bow

sometimes i watch netflix for the news
old dynasties, their bellies bloated, aswirl
flamboyant costume, the desperate masks
all the preening princelings smelling blood

the petty poseurs we are faced with these days
the son-in-law, the daughter, the many wives
the messiness of it all, the lack of character
mere hams on stage tearing down the scene

my hand wet and cold, i hold an icy drink
the sip of lethe that i permit, an easement of my way
through the slip of age, past the snip of youth
my mind warm and sharp, i hold it to the hot

i maunder as a pastime to talk to kin beyond
those that wonder sometimes what lies at inner core
those that choose to hold time cradled in their palms
that pack away a dwell time, to hold the moment more

i was asked to sweep the floor, look busy
the other tech, the long term man
he should do it because it's his long time job
you're just temporary and he will always be here

we need him, but would just like to say
you wire up pretty, and it all works the first time
we've never had that before, you're good
and you've already made our quota this month

i herd my wily cats, those stealthy thoughts
the complexity of memory purring ease
the solid beginnings of song on my lips, the need to record
with this new trigger from a shard of holistic memory

but finding the means, pen, paper, opening a new file
loses it, that holistic feeling pinned with just the right words
that triggers reformation of the memory
that on-switch, that recall and muse switch, gone

a restless wind in these first few days of april
spring late this year and warmth still missing
limbs unleaved toss their slim lithe tendrils
the restless mind wanders and yet remains

i sit in my study, sing to myself the moment
tap out a rhythm with my fingers
mind unleashed with the best new words
thumping the gourd of reality for deepness of tone

ransom notes can pinpoint worth
punch holes in plump balloon of place
prick fancied fantasies of love
but could never ever match your grace

nor push value farther by a farthing
the pride of bearing on your face
your worth is time, you fill its sails
leave wake that seeds a curling lace

memory wriggles the brain of my oak floor
holds up this self in its polished shine
bare foot spraddles toward the morning door
hand stoops to papers, thoughts to mine

coffee brings to focus a clear way ahead
toast, cheese, and olives with their briny touch
i know there could be many other lives instead
but then i never craved, nor saved, too much

i sit at the edge of a storm
i sit in a chamber of dreams
the winds in my mind butter warm
the blend of the coffee and toast

the bedroom of sunrise is awesome
the sun after rain unexplained
the draft of what's left is still pouring
i sip in delight what i've gained

my ship has docked, the luggage cleared
i struggle home to peace at last
my wants are few these last few days
my goals in sight, all milestones passed

my shoes are worn, their leather soft
i walk around each day i wake
my haunts are warm as winter comes
with snow and ice on road i take

the swooping bird, the mocking bird
atwitter with all his songs
and again from tippy top of tree
another, a better, melody

my morning walk to greet the news
the dawn of all that is to come
made graceful now for me
in tree and bird, song and glee

three quatrains

old men of power lose their edge, their nose
that wind-blown scent of what lurks out there
when half-turn to meet means all the world
when new wave coming can be last of waves

old men of riches lose their lust, their fire
that feral anger to touch and taste it all
that full-blown feasting on other's lives
they build a tomb and are buried there

old men of wisdom lose their faith, their hope
that trusting search for full set of answers
when what they face is loss of the world
which turns attention to what is left

i remember listening to a special one
chosen by our mothers to speak to us all
his eyes had the glitter of just having won
just having thought of the truth that he told

he apologized for bringing this power to his saying
he knew it was asking for the best ears we had
best eyes, best nose, best mind we had brought there
to the place where he was, we were all in his thrall

i knew then i'd made it far back, enough
to feel what my father's had felt in their time
how special such strength is when it's given
how precious his gift to us all

death song 27

i no longer swim into an ocean of future
weakened arms can only manage a smallish lake
and that if winds are calm and waves welcome
a foreshortened swim is all that's left

the second haying is dim in my past
the leaves all gone and snow on the way
weather bleak and sun on the wane
youth become the embers of age

i ache when i walk but persist in my walking
i wake with the sun, sleep when it's sleeping
my days half memory, half fullness of seeking
a blossoming gift each moment of being

death song 30

sore moves this winter down
this fortnight yet to know the same
i am born again next week
and crawl on icy hills yet still

another storm has come, still stays
i long for first things fresh again
in dream of calm, and balmy days
which still await mind's knife

which cuts to quick to see
what it is disturbs me so
it's what this now does show
this cold permanence of snow

so i just had my whiskey breakfast
wednesday morning with the medicine priest
the one for whom i kept his fire
a grey day, a little buzzed, looking out the window

we told old stories and laughed
how foolish we were when young
how wise we have become in our dotage
what fools we still yet will be

i don't know what will come next
nor did i know better back then
yet, i have survived until this moment
this far, indomitable, with a firm will to live

death song 21

the dime of death short stops us all
the tracks to follow disappear
there comes this impenetrable wall
beyond which lies nothing but fear

i talk, make noise to hide my guilt
alive and well, hurting but game
regarding future deeds still unbuilt
still on my focus, still on my game

but time has brought a fading crowd
those that i knew can't talk any more
gone to where i'm not yet allowed
the only thing left, the final score

words have a putative power
they catch hold of wind with their sting
twist it and coil it with meaning
and sometimes, even, they sing

they trill in the thrill of their curling
catch hands in their flexing of things
turn them and sand them to beauty
and sometimes, even, they ring

they pull with a mother's embracing
to smother what everything brings
tame it and twist it to full sense
and sometimes, even, they mean

fuzzywhumps and fizzigigs
how quaint my leaves are made of fog
how queer my downward creek will bend
as homeward seaward i will blend

fizzlefraps and whirlygogs
how won't i throw stones down to frogs
how will my flowers finely fade
how stone will turn to stone to jade

woogledyglues and things that stick
how sick am i of gate and lock
how well the water runs its stones
how seaward homeward bound my bones

we were herded together at harvard
us scholarship proles, there a week early
they lectured us, a welcoming lecture
of what we faced, and why we were there

it would be hard and would be enlightening
but the main effort should be for high grades
we the great unwashed thinkers from podunk
should eventually best all the prep school elite

our job was to validate the education
show how polished the gems of its genesis
so those privileged sons of those rich ones
could glide under the umbrella we raised

translation is misunderstood
think of it more as a return poem
the chinese gentry loved to play fun
they wrote careful lyrics, wrote carefully back

the rhymes would be the same
the sense come awry and poignant
an embellishment or homage
all just the grit of talk between the scholars

a necessary skill this protocol politeness
to be welcome to the soirees, the banter
or so i wish it were when i dream
i dream of being alive and learn'ed back then

there is a difference
a buffer between
back then, and what i am now
this recorder of dim past days

there is a vastness
a universal void within
the i am of what i wished to be
and the best of what i tried to know

there is an otherness
an around the corner way out there
the where we all are meant to go
the shared thoroughness of that trip

scales fall from rheumy eyes of evening
the mirror beyond glasses glistens its tale
marks left by the years glow manifest
carved by determined careen through life

stubbly beard speckled grey to white
cheek bones flush with angularity
lips still full but pursed with thought
tendoned neck a turkey wattle

gone the too slim scowl of anxious teen
gone the careful mask of knowing strength
gone the open grin of full-blown pleasure
yet hinting them all in memory's bin

old things come back, unbidden, whole
from nowhere now, from way back when
details astound, the taste, the feel
the fullness of the memory's tale

it happens more as i get old, the child
returns to visit in his wondrous ways
adamant in learning, in finding out
to get the wisdom in all the books

except i write them now, to fill the page
with rhythmic sounds of meaning
the more i catch, the more they come
their scratching d j screaming

my mind is trained, it seeks the why
it sniffs around to prove to self
the rightness of the thought
the whatness of phenomena

it tells me sometimes, what it thinks
to itself it makes passing mention
to pack memory's storage
with the howness of things

then imagining the why it is
puts action to the knowing
makes practiced way of doing
makes background seeking sharper, and on i go

it's a stately sail in this soft breeze
relaxed yacht of self in stride
a strangely warm november sun
the blue no cloud could ever tame

the earth is cursed with chaos though
splinter of future gone off, amok
the round of normal seasons strayed
a pleasant day when this land needs cold

the simple plants to change, to die
the more complex to molt, to sleep
and i, myself, to bundle self
to muffle close the seeds of spring

i've come to the time of departure
and seeing my friends disappear
not wishing myself to be burden
seeking exit, muted, demure

the leaving this party of life
should be quick, decisive, and clean
not drawn out, extensive, but sudden
a wave of the hand, a quick gulp of beer

the image behind such a closure
not sadness prolonged, not sun's setting
not twilight to ease end of day
just a snapshot, focused, and clear

i, I, eye, aye

i, I, and eye agree
and all nod their aye to me
there is no little, there is no big
there is no i, there is no me

the fund of sages all agree
big is where the big bucks come
and not to poets casting eye
to words of ink in forming i

the I of big is what i'm not
the i of smallness what i've got
the selfless self of i be heard
when i, I, and eye nod aye

i have now to decide, maintenance or joy
i'm old, falling apart, prolongation or pleasure
see the doctor, clean the teeth, or go to the bar
i seek the old remedies, to relax, quit hurting

there's not much left for me to spend
energy gone in the seedling of youth
pushed through its flower to seed once again
to pass on what wisdom time has allowed

that's what is left, the sense of it all
the reason of reasons, a changeless of end
self working for selfness, the self that you bring
it manifests knowing, at last, and full proud

fug of tobacco tastes the room
settles time within its cloud
allows an ease of rambling concern
heightens the sense of alcohol's bite

old cuban men sit in their preferment
sip old rum, watch the rain
nothing is rushed, not even the wind
bringing the clouds soaking the air

old cuban men without their senoras
seize the life they left far behind
taste the room abiding their being
smell the changeless future they find

dull red the brick of my back-yard wall
green grass, blue sky, sprinkled with clouds
but dreams last night were grim with danger
twisted sheets of morning my only clue

i know i'm anxious, angry for nothing
angry for everything, especially at night
the pause of easement is not contentment
there is no peace in calming down

suffering i see is suffering i share
the longer i live the shorter the future
not just for me but for those all around
the bitter truth, the truth of our ending

afloat on the calm baltic sea
on an island of plebeian pleasure
the ship offering a semblance of privilege
multitudes proud to have made it this far

overly polite servers burnish the image
everywhere smiling, cleaning, standing, waiting
but poshness is posture, repetitive staging
second rate amusement free for the taking

how long must one pose as upper class clown
expecting uniqueness offered for cut rate fee
how many lines to stand in, in thronging
up to the portals of fast fading dreams

this night will open softly for my thrust
the same as butter melting on my toast
with feelings being warm, caressed, i trust
the welcome in the arms of charming host

i knuckle under exactly what you are
that clings in subtle heat that ebbs and flows
a turning flicker is the morning star
that always wraps her feet around my toes

i still don't know how well i now belong
to exactly where i know so well you are
i only know i know quite well your song
that trills and sings at night on my guitar

rain stains the silver of my soul
meshes with the paling mist of eye
day sweeps with a billow and a swirl
it glowers huddled deep within a sigh

i haven't gone to see my dad in years
i huddle here alone and slowly die
the second sun of life has dimmed within
and darkling night comes swiftly on the fly

i wonder yet where mountain top will stop
but flailing wings can't get me up that high
above the crags that snatch at breath of sky
the ever-flowing brush of blue in wind

totality of view slowly fills in
builds sharp points of color, broad curves of line
an harmonious whole, a vision of mine
remembered now as the fullness of then

there is the hill, there the creek in my mind
there trees in spring bloom, fruit not yet won
sun slowly rising, the day just begun
a young man preparing to leave it behind

best thoughts bear rethinking, again, and once more
the picture in memory is seen best as form
repeated in seeing it looms last as charm
bringing warmth to feelings in memory's store

the sacred heart of all i am
strikes sparks on swollen seas
the dark descends as waters crash
the beating waves of passing mes

i stare outside the shell i am
to failing light that i can seize
the last of time that i will have
come bringing new felicities

i seldom find the time just so
it floats away and vanishes
the way life does when all we know
is left behind, and all that is, finishes

the bridge goes up in fog
as down i grope by hand
down to the misty bog lands
where ground is quick of sand

i see my pathway dimming
down slow i pick my way
down to the misty lowlands
my voice carves out my way

to whisper with a lowness
of what i still have yet
deep bass of rumble talking
this moment and its bet

shifting grey is oblique sky
swift and sudden how we die
soft and sighing breathes the leaf
stealthy cancer gnaws beneath

tightly twisting coil of rope
twirls to inward death of hope
tersely shifts its sigh of breath
twists to scratch its itch of self

whilom wandering in my flight
wishing oddly for the night
willful sloping downward swirled
moving waters made the world

a circle runs within my mind
my thoughts are zig and zaggy
i chortle deep to bend and bind
my steps are jig, then jaggy

i rise in pride and strut full proud
my flesh is full and jiggly
it stretches bounce to echo loud
the more or less of wiggly

i squeeze as much as i can touch
my heaving sighs are tearing
they gruffle deep within my keep
my feelings and their daring

late summer green glistens
full fall comes but not yet here
i cling to the life i see flourish
while winter is not yet the fear

a balance of youth and of wisdom
who wouldn't make such a choice
and here it is, out this my window
giving thought the nowness of voice

i've been here before and i know it
this glorious late afternoon
i sit here and sing what i'm feeling
cold to come, but not so very soon

i've found a cave to hide within
a small window lets me see outside
though the view allowed is much too thin
my thoughts can soar both deep and wide

i stretch to find a lazy stance
that eases twist on tired old bones
though aches abound in last life's dance
i trust my words won't sink to moans

i love the fight and hate to lose
the small bit left for me to have
i love the fact that i can choose
the soft warm nest that is my salve

i slippery, eelily, watch all my spielery
matching my thoughts with my sense of the night
i sloppily, jollily, catch all my drollery
snatching the sense of the chase and the flight

wolligee, golligee, what is my collagen
the place that i learned the wrong from the right
iffigy, piffigy, all is periphery
spreading as always, and always my plight

i logic'lly, codgerly, curse all cajolery
ranting and raving, i fight, and i fight
i pledgic'lly, legibly, leave thinking ledgerly
left on this page is the pen and its might

faint glow of misty lights suffuse through glass
the lambence of your face is touching close
warmth creeps to lips through nerves to pass
to you, then back to me, to shiver through to toes

is finding flesh of other finding source of me
were all the skids so greased when i was young
and didn't know what it was i sought to be
and reached to rhythm that words will have when sung

was all that then so i could feel this now
begin to be the fullness of my part
touching with my hands the way i know
holding fast to share my beating heart

did i tell you today that i love you
were you with me in dreams i adore
are you holding as tightly as i am
holding close as the sea holds the shore

were you there when i saw you the last time
was the where with all proper esteem
do we dance in the palace as ballroom
or squeeze with our bellies asteam

are the stars out tonight in our dark thoughts
have dolphins slid soft next my bed
to nuzzle and touch as the morning
springs grey when it brings back the red

beauty must have a place that shows
its thrall onstage, enframed
its focused thrill of seeing
frozen and secure

beauty must have walls for it alone
its thrill of cage its bars
its breath, its room and space
natural, demure

beauty must have soil to grow
its stalk dug deep, installed
its proper place, feeling anchored
strong, steady, sure

a faux pas is chaos of water
that crawls through itself like a snake
an oddness repeated is pattern
flops have a heaven at stake

a quarter past sunrise is autumn
the kill done quick to the bone
the rhythm that beats is a tom tom
delivering its richness of tone

ten minutes til spring is the break up
that throbs in the mind as it flows
this movement brings fog every morning
that boggles, then goggles, then goes

two things at once seems normal
now that the mind sees its end
an increasing iota of purpose
and nowhere a letter to send

three was when i used to be idling
chatting, or boozing with friends
but four was the usual purring
the lope that would last past all bends

six or seven often, when i was laughing
the self in a full body swirl
out to the bottoms of nowhere
where the tops of the trees love their squirrels

four quatrains

how imagine an ancestor you've never known
how see the stars embedded in their sparkle
how feel the roots that hold you to this earth
how sing the taste of love's tart sting

except as déjà vu, in echo of fresh tongue's phrase
except in darkest night enwrapped in inward sight
mid the tangle to those whose roots you share
except as darting child with his wilding

how might the mayan light his caves of tomorrow
how might the first hour fill the belly of today
how might the odd new leaf reach the widest branch
how might the tones enhance the daring leap

staring down into the very fundament
to sate the thirst for fail safe certitude
to bare oneself to sun in selfless churning
to find the swirling depths in tidal reefs

how imagine an ancestor you've never known
except as déjà vu, in echo of fresh tongue's phrase
how might the mayan light his caves of tomorrow
staring down into the very fundament

how see the stars embedded in their sparkle
except in darkest night enwrapped in inward sight
how might the first hour fill the belly of today
to sate the thirst for fail safe certitude

how feel the roots that hold you to this earth
mid the tangle to those whose roots you share
how might the odd new leaf reach the widest branch
to bare oneself to sun in selfless churning

how sing the taste of love's tart sting
except as darting child with his wilding
how might the tones enhance the daring leap
to find the swirling depths in tidal reefs

salty slush of urban snow
wets the boots of where i go
gusty wind stings face i know
woe enough for such as me

my father died this sunday last
no longer mine his voice of past
the forward now is what i cast
i talk as though it's what i see

this plodding gait is cold award
and somehow all i can record
i have no elder still on guard
now it's i who will be free

all directions seem somehow wrong
life become this bitter song
i wander, cold; oh, how long is long
this all that's left for me to be

the focusing on markovian connections
fills my opaque stare with working lattice
to hang my fleeting moments in the air
so they can sweetly dry to thoughts remembered

the fingers of the hand lead thought
the gestures of the mind take form
the language that we use is song
a train of reason time has wrought

time and attention brings it's order
the fingers know right down to bone
which is first, which is the following other
whose is ta-dum the drum of the heart

the marvel of how it all matters
to know that attention is key to it all
the testing of all that one's seeing
to grip hard with ink's splatter of scrawl

i reorganize the world in the mornings
when i sit and slip inside my mind
my strategies to fix things always work
if i could only gain the world's attention

but there is i think only one true world
inside the delicate mechanism which is me
and it only knows what it thinks it knows
what it conjures from complexities

a compressed world leaving ripplets behind
to slowly melt and fuse into the past
that part one holds yet of what one was
stored in that fallible system of memory facts

that's where i am when i do anything
aware only of what it is i think i'm being
aware, inside, where importance lies
the continuance of my many acts

mist wet of cold is wind
damp of breath bites deep inside
concrete step slaps sharp my footfall
green of grass gone dim, recalled

spring of limb was all in running
jumping push was hard, headlong
rush to win was bone contusion
life was fierceness of my song

hand tingles now its cold involvement
with burden held against its fall
my key opens new to warmness
behind, inside, within the walls

touch of life is still my springtime
thumping through its thrill of change
rushing fresh in new confusion
the never boring future strange

the summer seems indian in its soft intent
this afternoon seethes with its balmy breeze
not long from now will start the cold
the coming stillness of last desperate sun

i wonder why the ending starts so soon
what is the way that one ends one's song
when water growth of heat and tongue
will lick the skillet that sautés bones

that tries out the blubber beneath whale skin
that renders the oil that's fine in film
that rubs so slick and soft it's sin
to even hint one wants to win

and be forever this lovely day
that presages dates to come my way
the best of this, the last of that
the silver cup reflecting hairs of gray

a terrible wetness of late afternoon
comes crackling and crashing, comes blackened as doom
comes sleeting and hailing, an awkward monsoon
protecting my head i escape to my room

i stare out my window to trees as they fling
the winds and the torment now distant through glass
i wonder to self if i ever might sing
such feeling to climax, such feeling to bloom

an implacable storm outside my watch
a buffet of place both cold-hard and wet
i wonder what it is to stay dry, and warm
in feeling of comfort, in feeling of swoon

i shake my head to find other thoughts
mined deep within my imagery store
i wonder again at metrical fencing
to hold thought exact to where it is aimed

the heat is pregnant, its music sultry
this oppressive summer goes on and on
the leaden clouds invert a grey cool stratosphere
and shade the plains of this my world

i wonder if some other life might have been mine
if i had turned left instead of right that time
so long ago when the personhood that changed me
rose up in its verisimilitude

my children then would not be now
my wrist not have its well known ache
my head would be untrammeled then
and my passage here have calm its wake

i wonder if this hard edged life
that's right and all that's left to me
the little time that i have left
could raise in me an attitude

i thought that once was all i had
til what i had was all i knew
the crowded aisle of giving
the push of glass, the sip of dew

i thought the past was gone
til washing glass refilled my taste
made milling crowd the what is new
made smallness of the sip the waste

i wash my cup of wine with then
the where the all begins again
the where it is when all we know
descends upon the world as rain

i think anew the nonce of when
the what i have within my hand
the proud of feeling what i know
the sip, the taste, and now i go

my cave has light these lately evenings
midst glimmering ghosts of bright noon sun
they matter most as bands of color
knitting each moment into the one

my cave is plush these slow warm mornings
those leisure lumps of time my own
the buttered toast of appetite, news
brought just outside the door for me alone

my cake tastes sweet when i'm at table
the stiffening ache in every bone
the slathering feast of candlelight
steeping high tea to taste full blown

my cares are light with a habit of doing
small daily chores of sharing the load
the beauty of gift full in the effort
the baking of shyness to an inky code

dark morning sky is thick with cloud
stretched tight to cover me
forward gaze, unblinking, proud
unknotting ropes of duty now

sun, though up, is yet unseen
light altered, slowed, diffused
as are my thoughts of ends these days
strong, awkward, and confused

so empty of a reasonable choice
is life when it is gone
and what is real is real
remembered firm as bone

i choose to know what i can know
and let transpire the what-new now
til it becomes dumb mummer's show
and the quenching of my fire

this winter is snow, mist, and storm
i see through the window's clear grace
how safe is inside, and how warm

the world gives me time now to see
to sit through the days quite alone
my children are snowflakes and free
and i hate to call on the phone

this winter has been here before
and sunshine will come back again
i see through my mind's inner eye
both what is, and what might have been

my future is pale though, and thin
while memory is firm now, and sure
this day when i look close within
inside where it's warm and secure

slanted shadow flickers through bus window
the afternoon lengthens into night
sun of splendor reddens in its leaving
the city blossoms, muscled in my sight

the clatter homeward jumbles all our thinking
we cling to early summer, it becomes
a slow involvement seeking its own level
an energy felt as city's hum

i think of self as each of us do always
the self alone that each of us can feel
it shows in glint that lights impassioned faces
it settles here, then there, to set its seal

a happenstance enlightens happy children
an awkward grin becomes remembered charm
i think of those who slow, become their essence
unthinking afternoon imposes form

a wholesome heart weathers the rain
twisting its beats to find new tune
though never giving way too soon
before throbbing lightning brings fresh pain

a wholesome tongue labors to spell the truth
twisting its tip in a fricative drive
to parse the words so they're alive
with wisdom's bite, with wisdom's tooth

a wholesome hand will frame the door
hinge its gate to a stately gape
solid and there in its welcome shape
made fast; then loose to welcome more

a wholesome nose will sense fresh food
inhaling the bubbling stew of meat
the animal gone so you can eat
its life as yours in brotherhood

a woven warp of dimness lies across my bed this night
discursive woof of print on page now snags my jaundiced eye
i, once more startled, try to find the inner cloth of me
the blanket warms my open pores, unbidden comes a sigh

the focused gaze full inward turns as hands go slack in pose
glasses chewed around their stems taste new of thoughts grown old
this night of nights alone i seek the truths arranged in rows
of mildewed words, and slackened days, of youth so recent sold

i track my mind, its memories hold within my guts of fear
my home has firm foundation embedded deep in sand
i hold to life which slips away so slowly beer by beer
a book in bed and shelves still full await my palsied hand

i see the buck, the dauntless lad, who fought the heedless foe
who backed his thoughts with blood and bone
while always stubbing toe, who clung to words
though their porous web was always seeping sand
is this the way, recumbent way, he finally proves a man

beware the poet in his cups
who lurks in wait
to spring in hate
and squash cigars in beer

beware the poet in his lust
who hunts to mate
and writes his fate
in soggy, floating fear

beware the poet when he must
sizzle soon and late
and never be sedate
when he hovers by your ear

and

beware the poet and his gifts
in steady print ornate
which ever lies in state
in memory of this year

quiddity jibbety, then equanimity
a fair imbroglio, a fisticuff fight
harrity jarrity, all is hilarity
an amusing faux pas or a tryst in the night

flibberty, jibberty, then serendipity
a surprising sobriety, a stripe on the sleeve
parity, squarity, nothing is rarity
some things are for real and some make believe

topic'lly, follic'ly, then a full fashioned frolicky
a stubble, a stumble, a scent on the breeze
radic'lly, fadic'lly, then asininity
a suspicious society, then do as you please

sceptic'lly, kleptic'lly, then parsimonity
an edit, a snipping, a paring to bone
rapidly, sapidly, then inaninity
a pleasureful purpose, in a crowd or alone

the pen i wield captures me
it delimits what i feel
to what the ink allows to be
inchoate things congeal

entirety cannot be seen
the mind assorts its parts
allows within a sliver thin
enough for partial charts

details fine escape the net
swirl back in roiling sea
beyond my reaching get
without my boundary

all i am springs from these five
taste and sight, and always smell
touch and sound, they're all alive
and this inky streak as well

the sound it is which thrills as thought
and shapes it to its end
surprising with its formal lilt
its sense and sound ablend

the hand it is which forms the streak
and crablike makes its snake
coiling with its deadly threat
its wit and bite at stake

the mind it is controls it all
as habit guides its math
greasing slick the slalom trail
in well formed ice of path

the muse behind the stab at truth
advances past her veil
tempting sure the poet's will
to fill his ego's sail

water pools despite one's caring
the abyss welcomes what it wants
liquid thought lies deep down under
neon lights a house that haunts

blowing winds will take one's feelings
the ocean tides recall the soul
stony mountain thrust up yonder
shooting stars to point to goal

scorching sun will sear one's seeing
the desert bake until you're done
cotton tongue sit thick and useless
waking dreams in mind that's gone

starry night will shrink the ego
darkest thoughts shoot through and through
silver moon-beams, lambent, streaming
your beating heart the all of you

early light, mist rising, down to water's edge
look out on ceaseless moving, wet my hand
i know this place, it's always new, i stand
so slips within my mind the thinnest wedge

a shim so deftly placed glides softly then
bursts in understanding dawn is day
a pry to loosen tongue so i can say
raucous things with this, my rooster pen

but world around still, still fast abed
a snoring ignorance of fresh dim light, of birth
reaching sudden down from eastern tip of earth
above me now, me deep alone in head

kind world allows to life a struggling wrath
in turn again to climb along the way
nodding slowly inward, giving senses play
going patient home on well worn path

dull color of sleet is my face
this winter of snow, mist, and storm
i see through the window's clear grace
how safe is inside, and how warm

the world gives me time now to see
to sit through the days quite alone
my children are snowflakes and free
and i hate to call on the phone

this winter has been here before
but sunshine will come back again
i see through mind's inner eye
what is, and what might have been

my future is pale though, and thin
while memory is firm now, and sure
this day when i look close within
inside where it's warm and secure

there's a peculiar problem in man's most
modern particular thought. it has become
pertinent and to the point, quite lost
in the thicket of its quick flooded sum

the left becomes wild way to ideate
the right becomes a cascading spate
where down is blown froth of water's way
and up is where you look in your dreaming play

the down i see when my eyes see yours
reflects the heights i must show to you
for in the flecks of your quick sure peeks
glint the flooding touch which your body speaks

i search for depths in every way i know
i search for ground for my soul to touch
you give to me, soft, resilient, slow
you give to me a particular much

i looked around and knew at once
and licked to taste the smell of you
that now i dreamed a great true dream
that had now happened and was now true

you were the warmth of sun i saw
you were the trees and grass and dew
that sparkled red at break of day
you were the night, the whole night through

and if i chose to end this scene
(for dream it was and this i knew)
your snuggled warmth was there for me
your laugh and touch were all my due

but not right then did i awake
i nestled down where all was new
thought and saw and touched a world
that turquoise shows with its sky blue

the cardinal swooped down into the yard
then high up within the bordering trees
and called to see what might be the answer
i listening hard heard only bees

again the call, again the wait
deep thoughts began to slowly stir
and pop in mind as soap suds will
my skew of mind began to purr

the sunlit lawn was limned in song
the flowers danced as gusts came down
and cooled my sweating chest at rest
the song again bounced all around

i reached out straight and touched the air
my feet held fast to the ground alone
my ears were tuned to this other where
and he called his love in trilling tone

the summer seems indian in its soft intent
the afternoon soothes with a balmy breeze
the coming weakness of low southern sun
not long from now will start the cold

i wonder why the ending starts so soon
what is the way one ends one's song
when water growth of heat and tongue
still licks the skillet that sautés bones

tries out blubber beneath whale skin
renders the oil so fine in film
it rubs so slick and soft it's sin
to even hint one wants to win

and be forever this lovely day
the breath of life now come this way
the best of this, the last of that
the cup of wine, fire hardened clay

a baboon circling the meadows
i skulk about in trees
look down at all my kind
the ones i wish to join

young, ambitious, frustrated
the women all down there
with that stony old bastard tony
the one who tops them all

practice craft, work on strengths
prepare to erupt, sudden as steam
finally attack the brute
the one that must be beaten

ready as will ever be
all is inner pride
chivy heart, risk it all
take my place among the women

do little i know anything
was little i there
did the dark deed happen
do little i care

i sit in municipal appeals
to betterment
i watch citizen's squirming
bewilderment

do big I Know Anything
do big I Care
did the Axe Fall When Dropped
was big I There

am i hanging now
for the deed
I was Thinking so
i must bleed

i am but a man, and i have two feet
twenty fingers and toes, one head
orifice three or four, who counts
no different from all such folks

i walked with both dignity and pride
a man with deep thoughts and feelings
a pony-tail, scraggly beard, as i might
adorn myself, stubbornly idiosyncratic

i talked with both poise and surprise
a man with early training and polish
suited up, ironed shirts and a tie, i tried
stiffly polite projection of competence

i balked at both blather and blame
with a sly witty way with my words
ink stained, squinty-eyed, i posed
a laughing clown my honed weapon of choice

i became a river of voices
those striving to learn while they stared
straight and with eyes that were open
as their throats trilled to ancient advice

be there when the happening happens
hop quick when the slither slides home
note all as you laughingly saunter
through lithe brand of life of the young

i told all those rapid beseechings
the classes, the ones that i taught
i told what i've always had, feelings
i quivered my arrows in heart

they learned from my solemn expressing
that life has a soul and it's hard
i remember the joy of their passing
the gates of their hands weaving strings

i came home to the clean house
fresh scrubbed by the venezuelan
fresh smell of pinesol fumes
apartment aglow in afternoon sun

new york, cause that's where it is
remade time, time and again
encrusted hard venues in its heart
never the same, the dao of these times

river still there, off in the distance
leaves not yet gone, outside a window
but fall is here, the start of cold end
ever the same, inside of cold earth

home still dry, still warm, still here
things to do and do again, fresh starts
but winter comes, so i store the good things
food and firewood, those things that one needs

i fly above the cares of the world
the ocean below, vast, churning, deep
a small head wind, no turbulence to feel
i sit awake with no desire to sleep

it's seldom enough i escape this high
nothing but idleness and odd thought
i can escape and go walkabout this while
zazen as discipline for such as i

soft murmur of eating, deep throb of the jets
soundscape devoid of sex songs of birds
a limited view of seat backs and curtains
the business of travel a cocooned wait

family behind and more family ahead
a few hours release from a lifetime of effort
wherein i chose to eschew imperial grace
to walk the side-path of no recognition

i hear a crickle in the fluorescent lights
and a humming whirr that stirs the air
a stern old clock ticks time away
there is no window to this modern cave

i push the paper from around my mouse
and squint to see computer screen
my wrist winces as i pound the keys
to make memory of my fresh made thoughts

i pause to hear my own breath pulse
i touch my chin and stubble reminds
how i keep changing despite this place
its sterile square portentous space

i pinch my nose and stroke my hair
take off my shoes and wiggle toes
i try to imagine a grassy field
the sun and water, some other where

i know the circles of heaven
and the sun is finally turning north
every morning more so
a little longer it will light my way

but dim and grey is what the cold is
water caught and made opaque
in crustal wonder of its magic
til life and warmth is thawed, reborn

i know this mist and all its coughing
its clammy grasp in throat, its rasp
it yields to brightness, color wrapping
a bird in feather red to glow

i know the summer lies off yonder
know that heat will sweat, and i will curse
the very day i wished for sunshine
to hurry back and make things green

i learned enough to gather food
greens, onions, fish, rabbits, squirrels
i had to pay attention way back then
we all needed enough for us to eat

those days now gone, long gone before
i have lost my patience, my quietude
i skip to the end of magazines, of videos
i know most of the stories, not all the endings

i wonder when this new phase set in
when my kids grew up and went on their way?
when the aches and tiredness came quick and fast?
when the world itself seemed to explode?

i remember when the slow ease of current
mesmerized, brought soothing serenity
i remember the last end of the fire
we quenched before we packed on out

i still cook the careful meals
and eat, and drink as old
but miss the murmur of the joy
in your gnashing swirl of fill

the music in the background
now only makes me old
not young in dance of song
when i warbled to your trill

i miss you every morning
that wakes up with you gone
the coffee seeming endless
the days last twice as long

please come back home tomorrow
the child within me says
watches outside slowly
through the windows in his days

is my practice now my purpose
have i lost where i began
have my muscles made my memory
are my thoughts within my hands

have i seen by memory's touchings
have i counted one, two, three
are my feelings softly holdings
are my tastes sweet honey tea

is my practice not my purpose
have i not gained rhythmic time
have i not forged molten newness
picked apart each finger's rhyme

have i not sensed digit's holdings
have i not found pattern's worth
are not my tellings touching
my songs from rooster's perch

legs become more leaden than not
goal not yet in sight, but surely on the way
in morning cool, the sun still beating proud
i walk to see and feel the urban wild surround

eyes blurred enough to birth a squint
books i haven't read, those piled around my chair
in coziness of room, the thoughts still there, in spate
i sit to ponder memories that so beguile

teeth sore and chipped, but holding up as yet
food i've yet to cook, to feed the crew around
in kitchen warmth of smell, the food which died for me
i cook some every day to satisfy and fill

blood slowing down its pressure, but pumping right along
with proper balanced lifeforms, the why i'm still around
in pleasant living quarters, the cluttered sidewalk near
here to live by river's richness the balance of my days

my father told me about memory
it was when he showed me the camera
how its memory was total and complete
just for that fleeting exactment of time

he said my job was to brain remember
and to do it with all the tools out there
but basically brain memory since it is always at hand
if practiced and worked at like mimicry

he remembered episodically as we all do
and ordered associatively, by small exact correspondence
some trigger to the fullness of the past
to the tale telling exactness of the complex story

that's what we have left, photographs
and written translations of memories
some shards of windows into his life
brief glimpses of stories he left part told

sadness bursts through the dunes
roils the streets with its rivers
a mississippi of wetness
there is no song to match these tears

but the world knows i will have tried
as do barking seals beg their treat of fish
this is not humdrum everyday, this is now
a doomsday come real, a havoc for our time

the natural has shown it can do all of this
cast cars spinning into oily heaps
lift tankers bodily onto shore roads
bring rivers to drown our basements

there is nowhere to hide from this tide
it is relentless, driven by wind and moon
there is no room left for regrets
the ocean has come to the streets of our homes

my ultimate god like my ultimate father
lives in the ear of my speech
the song recognized as crucial to core
the statutes of memory hard-wired

my words resonate in their chamber
rich with accretions' patient arrays
underground, hidden til the bloom of their days
caught out in the light giving birth

they slither black on white expanse
to shimmer in their colors
they shape the mind in inner sight
evoking primal glimpse

they leap to life in moment's tone
erased to all but inner cache
of thoughts that itch their way to top
ready for the mind to scratch

now let's see how inky the streak
when it becomes the ebon we crave
when we are wont to scribble amok
in carefully prepared canvases shown

now let's hear how smoky the sound
when it becomes the veil of our heart
when we are wont to vibrate our being
in throb of ecstasy moving the air

now let's feel how soothing the stroke
when finger's grip in a softness of touch
when we are wont to cradle the other
in warmth of life-gift, in mothering care

now let's sense how unbridled the freedom
when we are wont to open the mind
when it becomes a truth searching way
to smile to the understanding world

roiling clouds bedaub with grey
in swirlish stain of passing
sit beneath this shuttered light
this friday everlasting

seek outside this cell of now
this hellish chain held tightly
full faced time in life's embrace
this friday day of sorrow

slurp this night its veil of wetness
on this third, this fourth of same
the rat stink smell of dankness
flesh that ages clothes my bones

in liquid pooling sweat smell
the mind that will not settle
this ticking toll of heart beats
that lead on to tomorrow

the thing is, how hard do you push others away
like, try to remember: only two score years ago
it wasn't til 1978 that i could build a fire
a fire to bring the spirit for all those gathered there

why did it take that long to allow us indians to be us
why did religious freedom extend to all others but us
the wildness, i suppose, the oogedy woogedy of spirits
the hallucinagenic drugs, the drunkenness, the vital spirit

it was fear of us which did us in, that and our land
they wanted that land and its free riches, to exploit
and did they, they tore it all away and excluded us
sent us to the worst of the land to wither and decay

that's how hard they pushed and threw us away
their fear of our feelings, our spirits, our ways
fear gave proof to their slaughter, made moral their cause
finally they grudging gave approval for me to build a fire

to me fear of death is always in the doing
the young who rush ahead with eager breath
the old who cling to slow walking ways
the middle who just wonder where it went

to me fear of love is always in the shyness
the young who hurt so painfully
the old who feel the loss of love the most
the middle who just wonder why it goes

to me the fear of pain is in the ruing
the young with owies waiting to be kissed
the old who want a peace and calm at ending
the middle who just wander through their days

to me the fear of trust is always in the slyness
the young who cheat their instincts to survive
the old who feel their worth grow grey, diminish
the middle who just muddle yet and still

trickster is medicine
masking true divinity of actual event
making palimpsest suffice for deed
an echo making sense of sound

rattle tent when a spirit walks by
inside believe what you believe
but confidence is the name of the game
and where it's bred it's found

a troubled soul seeks solidity
in a cleansing of the sense of shame
the bulbous prick of goat skin flailed
by ugly grotesque friendly clown

the song itself begins as frail
as palsies of the normal brain
then grunts and snorts, and then the fool
puts wayward feet back on the ground

try to carve out a place for your self
where you can simply relax and be
but not a place of ease and rest
quiet, yes, but all in all a busyness

a time for a wandering mind to roam
and space to pace in the thinking of
not truly a place of calm quietude
so much as a creative solitude

to search the self for its wanton vibes
its really want to know, its guts
but not a place of frenzied haste
so much as a splendor of certitude

to weigh understood possibilities
to heft the data field and then decide
in that older place, the place of elders
with the certainty this last is final

words, the twisting maze of chosen way
the hedge of hemming in the moment
limiting sense to loosen the thought
in focused meander through the whole

sounds, the whirling world around the maze
the rhythm a living heart beat song
feelings set loose to freely dance
in sensuous moving of the soul

shape, the sideways scrawl of meaning
the idiosyncrasy of the final form
the deeper truths beneath, to find
by peeling the bark to heart of tree

voice, the primal source of different being
the articulation of the inner world
communicating what the self won't know
til hand makes real in inky trail, to show

you carry the world with you
wherever you go, whatever you do
you are part of her who birthed us all
all who share in her bounteous ways

and her tempers, she's more important than us
when she snarls and floods our plains
burns trees, the homes in mountain forests
she needs our help, not our ignorance

we have to all live together, this earth world
the germs as well as the lions and wart hogs
the oscillation of the seasons, their turmoil
their beauty and passion, their hardship

it all has reason when we become the earth herself
when we accept our stewardship of this world
when we admit to self, one and all, we must pull together
accept the strictures of a safer, diminished place

a rolling thunder comes my way
spreading a slow blackness
a fitful wind matches fractious mood
the heavens release a cleansing rain

here i sit and i must wait
a turbulence beset animal
for the cascade that water brings
roiling rivulets to rush away

here i sit for the time remaining
hungry for an easement, thirsty for the rain
eager for involvement in natural change
ready for the denouement, here i sit

lightning strikes a hundred yards north
then dead calm, and hair stands on end
a crack to the west and rumble overhead
when will life happen, what more will it bring

76 to the chinese

i guess i turned out to be what i wanted
someone who gave, learned, appreciated
especially the learning, the paying attention
memories are all i really have to pass down

the chinese say we all die before a hundred
that at least is how it used to be
i'm well on my way and still passing down
the what i gleaned by passing through

three quarters of the way there
six bits and still counting
well past the due date of most humans
differentiable us all, all people

i've wandered a peculiar, individual way
scarred and feathered by what i've done
now for me it's the doddering dance of age
grandly done on a soft lit stage

an orange cast to the bricks across the way
a slow dimming of the life bringing light
a palpable link to majestic sun's decay
i sit silent while city shivers into night

day of brilliance slowly fades in grace
a gift of knowing what love can sing
i sit and watch from depths of spring
singing soft words from a special place

time lengthens as one thought lingers
now ends the magic of this moment's brush
i touch hair and teasing twirl my fingers
the breeze itself keeps saying shush

i do, i let my scrawl end this rhyme
then sitting still my soul takes flight
it stands, then leaps, and roars its might
colors memory in a measured time

five or more quatrains

i nod in ease and know i'll sleep
the moment i choose to let go
i sip the wine that's always there
when life is full with meaning

the truth to tell is always hard
and fraught with double meanings
the simple truths of you and me
both frail, and fraught with yearnings

this night is cool with fitful breeze
i slow to fit its silence
the legacy you leave behind
is love unloosed and warming

i can't full speak the what i know
i can't hold tight full feeling
i can although with lithesome stroke
limn love that highlights being

to hair, to eyes, to costumed flow
of dancer's body yearning
i watch with love and touch to know
communicate life's burning

a cooling breeze and clear bright day
and yet it brings no jolt, no joy
the empty center of my mind obtrudes
i miss my little girl, my sprouting boy

i know enough to be alone
i know they need their place to live
to be somewhere i seldom go
i know again nowhere to give

this day dawned bright so long ago
i wonder how it stretched this far
my work went fine, i felt ok
but eyes, i know, held vacant stare

non-seeing eyes, non-feeling hands
no smile to meet my other loves
i fumble now to right myself
i slowly peel my rubber gloves

i reach to touch my chest
and heartbeat thumps my freshened hand
i sit to think, and slowly change
rebuild life now on shifting sand

a spitting rain and fretful wind
spots the glass of this my seeing
blurs the edge of where i am
drives deep within my being

i slowly walk to think things through
and feel my essence stretching
my muscles warm with work well done
my thoughts of future-- guessing

the rush of time speeds through my days
there is no leisure as i run
snatching hard young grasping hands
in river flow that's never done

i wonder when was last i ate
i wonder what i'm feeling
and smile and see with inward light
how life has clouds not ceiling

i pause to think, decide to stop
and rest while waiting, drinking
a crawling scrawl of this my place
an ego steady, shrinking

a wholesome tongue labors to say the truth
twisting its tip in a fricative drive
to parse the words so they're alive
with wisdom's bite, with wisdom's tooth

a wholesome hand will frame the door
hinging its gate to a stately gape
solid and there in its welcome shape
made fast, then loose, to welcome more

a wholesome nose will sense fresh food
inhaling the bubbling stew of meat
the animal gone so you can eat
its life as yours in brotherhood

a wholesome heart will feel full deep
straightening true what words can't tell
a warm and giving, bottomless well
exact as rhyme, and made to keep

a wholesome man walks determined pace
bringing warmth of heart with his joyful song
his hands held tight, determined, strong
his eyes seeking windows to an other place

my daughter asked today when i will die
i wonder why she wants to know such things
i wonder, as she answers, "when your hair turns white"
why mine still clings to its dark brown state

i wonder why i cling to younger ways
than my flesh is wont in its age to do
i wonder why she wants to know such things
and i answer, "life has death as its first sure date"

i ask my son if what he wants to be
is still the same as it was yesterday
and it is, as engineer; and daughter wants
as daughters will-- money, fame, a movie fate

i look around, ask myself in quiet tones
if its fear or boredom will get me first
i wonder new my small-boy wondrous thoughts
of life, of love, of getting to stay up late

to talk to women and to learn it all
to learn how life can be short, full and sweet
how death might come tomorrow night
or be here right now, coming down the street

so what is rest for a marmot
asleep through the night in her bole
high in the crags of the mountains
with her acorns gathered and whole

her winter now stretches before her
as she fluffs her soft fur in her nest
what next should she do for tomorrow
is her life now to turn for the best

is she happy all snug in her dreaming
so deep that she doesn't recall
when waking in dark before dawning
of day that might promise her all

all the things she might wish for to happen
all the things she might leave now undone
the rest of the days that are shortened
then the long ones in hot baking sun

i wonder when thinking of her thoughts
what prompted the poise in her smile
as nestling she gives as she touches
and her being so warm all the while

the thought is difficult to entrain
the left is reflex, and the right
comes pounding thoughtful
and less than sure in its blind sight

skies are rich these days of welter
and sleep at all is dreamful dread
the waking toss in early morning
the tortured wrench of thinking head

the breeze exhaust of urban evening
booze and flounce in partnered rain
i love you the flowing body
dancing slave to gestural gain

rivers deep reach up from center
turn this night into a cage
barred without the fears of fencing
rippling to this end of page

did i once when first i told you
remind of how the saying is
that love is taste in all its nuance
the artful flick of garnish twist

death song 25

a child i was when old age began
i reached it all as i lived forward
as if to bend the ear, quietly
to learn, to search and find, to know

a youth i was when my strength was prime
i used it all as it passed me by
ravenous and new, in hunger
to taste, to feel and hear, to know

a man i was when i helped the best
i lived it all as it took my all
steadfast and strong, with honor
to serve, to change and grow, to know

an elder i now offset the rhythm
i rise to all, the dawn i have
slew foot and slow, always with wonder
to slurp, to suck and taste, to know

as not-yet dead, i still bring news
step out on stage, intone the truth
awkward and feeling, pealing with thunder
to stand, to teach and leave, to know

earth is testing me these days
cold wet october, warm november
thawing oceans in the northland
floating continents of ice in the south

the world is round and round it goes
the more you push the more she flows
in chaotic macrobursts of difference
that add inexorable heft of fact

this globe meanders in her plenitude
hiccups her grinding wrath of storm
bakes the tundra past its frostpan
down beneath to slush and sand

takes the caps from off the andes
sends the floods to tidal shores
makes the rivers mile wide sweepers
twisting, flooding all before

earth, the world, this globe, will do that
and yes i know she's willing yet
to give still more to those who scoff her
scarfing her bounty in careless ways

han shan   cold mountain

i found these old writings in a book
left in the corner by a grandfather from long ago
i let it talk again through the way i write
what i have gleaned from his bones of thought

a plain-spoken question was all his disguise
as far into the hills he climbed to his spot
he left small songs of what he was
how he had come to record his thought

acceptance of death, acceptance of life
the wordless land of feeling the all
full grandeur of what was outside his mind
seen, smelled, touched; heard and eaten

that was the norm of this man's being
alone, quiet, with time for no-thought
involved, there, accepting the world
sometimes wandering to visit old friends

i usually hide the thoughts i allow me
but when so disposed, i do jot them down
sing to myself as it's happening
enigmatic, true, and only my self

i was watching television in the ninth grade
in dallas texas, it was a fort worth channel
thirty miles away we could pick up the signal
we tuned the picture with the all-night signal

the mcarthy hearings, him and the army
he was a lying cheating son of a bitch
but it took a while for the truth to come out
his bluster and shout all that you read

we read papers back then
they brought us the news
they were owned by the rich
but they were basically straight

so when we, far-flung citizens could see
bombast and puffery skewered with truth
our faith in the nation sipped of the brew
the heady sense of family and pride

all symbols and folly of course
the privileged kept privilege quite close
obscured by the brilliance of stage craft
and sopranos who sing like the birds

memory is a fragile sense in modern times
sight and sound mechanical, digitalized
destroying the will to internalize and own
machines our hippocampus, discs our associations

new words to google, every keystroke magnetized
held fast only as long as electric, as long as decoder lasts
but what of how the human animal found its way
what of the arts of not so long ago

song and rhyme, pencil and oil
the long practice of words to indeliblize
what of the strengths we found so necessary before
what will be the forms of our new creations

thoughtless snapshots of a summer beach
quick videos of a baby crawling
tweets of ever fewer words
abbreviation instead of studied depth

no longer to hold a newspaper and read
no longer to turn the page in a book
the touch screen of idle conjecture the norm
the very shape of our future a finger's swipe

moccasins report concrete, unyielding
rains run swift into grated holes
roots are here in these squares of difference
deep in mind, nowhere else to go

fruits that form exit my fingers
pecking away at syntactic form
blinking light keeps the pathway
breathing words, unheard but seen

the world i knew and all it brought forth
gone long behind the change i've known
now i speak into a darkened future
a smaller world with narrowed ears

people hear what blares before them
sent loud and clear from corporate mind
deafness descends, defeats all magic
perverts my song and tears my voice

so i keep my eyes on words of power
that echo long in my heart their pain
but i can't tell this truth to others
who listen not to my silent rain

my first granddaughter is pugnacious
she wants to be the best and win
writes songs, plays, and sings
tastes it all in search for better knowing

my first grandson is the dreamy me
he cartoons hands with toons
reads history for agony of memory
tastes difference as a main course

my second granddaughter is the wild one
she wants to find her own way in life
imagines her own world as she plays
tastes always for the same foods

my second grandson is the bandy legged warrior
he wants to do the right things
tries to get everything that he can
tastes always for his favorite foods

four stair steps to the future
are made of part of me
they carry me forward
to see what i won't see

i want a primeval nose
that smells a pagan richness
i want a fertile land
that nurtures all my seed

i want a primeval eye
that sees through screen of danger
i want an autumn hue
that fills my barns of greed

i want primeval ears
that lend hands to guitar's song
i want a dance to set my mood
that bares my heart to bleed

i want a primeval touch
that soothes fur for neck to snuggle
i want a food that fills my longing
that feels thicker when i chew

i want a primeval taste
that tells what death still gives me
i want my meat to feast upon
that freshness in earth's blood

when i was a young man, an indian in the city
i dreamed a lot about slipping off into the woods
becoming a hermit as it were, a recluse
away from the tumult, the mastery of those others

the first policeman i ever saw was a game warden
we lived off the rivers a lot, had our own garden
we seined for the fish, tied our own nets
but they wanted to make sure we had a large mesh

they would come and inspect us, flashlights and all
a ruler to see the size of the square hole of the web
that let us catch the big fish so we shared what we got
too much for us and others had needs

and i wanted that life, the integrity of it all
me and the landscape, the forest, the birds
the small patch of garden, the summer fresh food
the hard tack of winter, the chewing, the waiting it out

i wanted all that, resplendent in my childish imaginings
but my way led into concrete, and the hardness that means
my feet crave the grasses, my eyes seek horizon
my hands wish to make and be busy, grow hard

now window of sight sees a gross squareness
caves that glare through the loud city nights
i shut my eyes to that brightness, that yammer
think back to that boy, and the river he loved

the words came flat and cold, unbidden
like the wind on raw spring days
a horse i knew is now unridden
i heard news grow hard in stony ways

but day is fresh and warm in welcome
though bus is late and people numb
i catch the slowness pacing fresh growth
the start begins with hand and thumb

the preparation for all that's coming
this time of growth, then that of death
to store to make it through til next time
it smells as sweet as water's breath

the coolness sprung from deep down under
subduction through the inner maze
a water-gift from earth our mother
seen soft as light through morning haze

i wandered quick from knowing stoppage
and image flowed to texas springs
and crisp, cool water in the dawning
the sense of life that loving brings

loving other so death is wrenching
the guts away, and in a wink
oh, how the self will rot, decay
and how this life is but a blink

179

i mention to you this morning the sadness i feel
at seeing the elbowing fight for scraps
at hearing the raised voices of anger directed into the circle
at smelling the rottenness of uncaring hearts

where are the ones whose pride stands tall
in stooping to help the ones that hurt
why are the children left all alone
to raise themselves from their playpen's dirt

why do i sing this sadness i feel
hearing the rain and not going out
why do i cry to wet my warm place
why do i not run out and shout

roar loud enough for all to hear
tell what i know, informative thought
erasing their fear of how we are wrong
different and wild so we've never been caught

except by ourselves in paying their price
of taking their alms in blank staring need
heeding their voice promising more
if only we water and flower their seed

i don't want to be another of them
and yet that is what i do so to live
i don't want to be so hollow inside
so i will build from within the all that i give

murphy at the niea conference 1989

the slow grey morning sits outside
i sit with coffee and no papers
no handy escape to large events
and sweeping forces to fall into

i sit with coffee and with my dreams
which persist in their reality
i sit with a pen and blank paper
a handy escape to sit inside

the slow grey morning seeps away
the full of cold is now inside
there is no heat to luxuriate
no sun of color to tan my hide

the slow grey morning reflects my thoughts
they're old and thick in their purpose
and blocked by years, and blocked again
but turning world insures a change

and change is the dappled horse we ride
into the teeth of slow grey morning
time of grief at the cold inside
that time will bring; and now i tell

i seek to dream and thus make real
it's hard enough sometimes to tell
exactly what it is i feel
and not have those i love recoil

i sit with coffee and this scribbled page
i've spent this time to spend my rage
in squiggling lines and muted thoughts
the slow grey morning becomes my me

the rexographs and pentiums
conflict before my eyes
the students swirl their teenage space
in childish exercise

i work amongst some grown up men
who never have to fight
nor carve a place from nature raw
with sinew and with might

i sometimes wish that i could be
some other place than here
some other place where realness is
and fear is really fear

some other place than prison halls
that lock the students in
some other thought than lesson plans
that plead for sense of sin

some other way of spending time
than rotely being numb
some other cage than passive walls
that make one deaf and dumb

i'm insular within this stream
that flows before my door
the waves that lap around my feet
come from another shore

some other culture i don't know
surrounds and closes in
some other people share my space
and drive me deep within

to memory's cave and drawings there
lit dim by flickering fire
to dancing senses, dreaming time/ at night when i retire

182

asian forms

in the old days, in china
they taught to memorize

in medieval times, in islam
they taught to memorize

in modern times america
we're taught to meme our eyes
into data distraction

at least those past elders could argue
the deep base of shared knowledge
today we flip through menus
respond to photos and don't expand
don't uncover thoughtful text first hidden

god help if poetry or other art intrude
the flowers of wordiness, the words that bloom
words should intrigue the mind of tongue
the language of each our difference
we should spin our tales
to achieve the slip of tideful ease of knowing

murphy living through a february of no snow

tsalagi 7 line

poetic forms are battlefields
they are fought over by those who care
and those who wish to be new and better
are often hamstrung by adherence to form

the sonnet is a cage in question
it has its rhythm and its rhyme
fourteen lines in two parts
an octet thought then response of six

if cut in half it might be better
more tsalagi if that's the theme
a quatrain fullness broad and thoughtful
a tercet short to answer...seven

the first example of what i call a tsalagi 7 line
basically a cut down version of the petrarchan sonnet 4 4 3 3
it's in my book medicine wheel by grandfather rattlesnake
that trickster name emblazoned on the amazon site

i got a buffalo nickel in my change today
the man's proud face worn to a blur by time
the beast loomed large as it always did
though its shag was smoothed by years gone by

this relic i found in this unsought way
was with a quarter, a penny, and a dime
to remind me fresh of sad past, sore hid

then i changed it to fit a chinese thought mode

buffalo	nickel	change	today
man	worn	blur	time
loom	beast	large	always
years	smooth	shag	gone

relic	found	unsought	way
with	quarter	penny	dime
sore	past	fresh	remind

more of the 7 line

i climbed the mountain of my life and am almost back down
all that up and down was my exercise, my being
i have said the same ever since the start, and patiently
now listen again--- my memory is getting bad

the moon is not yet full, but shimmer of lake fills it out
my eye's path to that moon below is direct
the sage of old says pay attention to the water

a wise woman taught me the craft of weaving
the threads of my life became a fibrous bundle of soul
now the wily daughters of earth spin beguiling truth
the green smell of grass, the fit of the turkey gobble

my hands breed pattern in the willows
shape all i see so i can live
i touch the earth with all her blessings

sometimes i go the long way around
i slow my pace and forget the time
the unusual path interests me
and i willingly wander its direction

how can i hear song resting in chord
how does echo teach the pond to flow
how add sound's sense to wordy flow

thoughts aren't thoughts until they're worded
strung out in a trail of embroidery
fine picked and colossal, detailed and vast
those words left us we should read

read best you can find of your own history
your own background of effort, your story
the story of your family lives on in you

water seeps into the ground
dissolves into the thirsty roots
lifts itself through tubal threads
spreads to leaf absorbing sun

moving not from chosen place
holding fast and growing tall
nest for birds, shade for all

little one who asks to come to wisdom
you vacillate: now wine, now pickles
i watched the fire last night in my wonder
at your becoming shrewd before you are wise

you won't give away your new eagle feather
and the drummers need their spirit gift
it's not you that owns that icon of virtue

for a while when i was young i prospered
for a while all i touched saw love
the end of my life, listen to what has happened
like a cloud i came, like a wind i become

and yes i reflect and yes it is all me
head drinking the glass i am everything in everything
and yes i am the water of life and the bowl carrying it

we are going to the orchard to sing, don't forget your guitar
bring along the water drum, we have won our war
we are alive and the taste of our time is our dancing
as the buck hares do in their coital stomp

we start as a boulder tumbling off a cliff
we smash down the shoulder of the mountain
we make a creek for the earth's sweet tears

i am the firekeeper who kindles the fire of truth
for repentance, for sin, for love, and for hate
i kindle a flame that sings as it cleanses
i am made of earth, you are part of my hearth

i went to the earth and entered her sweat lodge
my feelings were received with great good humor
the sweet grass fumes foamed on my skin

strip bare your heart, throw its clothes in the ditch
hide your face and think yourself born anew
a tadpole you must live only in water
let whatever come you must jump in the stream

i sat on the earth and felt that i knew her
she said you walk on your own two feet
i asked why she always pushed forward true reason

i can never know the truth of the earth's creation
yet it fills my heart with love and laughter
and how i tremble in the warm april breeze
flower stem flouncing, its head filled with color

any spot i lay my head on earth, she is the cushion
in all four directions, up and down, she is the center
gardens, flowers, bird songs, ecstasy and her

i lost all my odes and love poems to the water
all my clothes and belongings taken by the flood
now, all i am, good, bad, sensual, cherokee
comes from mother moon, and her sight takes me away

isolation is worth more than a thosand meetings
now, all i am, good, bad, sensual, tsalagi
comes from mother moon and her sight takes me away

the spirit which placed fire in my spirit
placed a hundred different fires on my tongue
i burn in all six directions, and i burn within
if i complain the spirit puts its hand over my mouth

the souls who know not the ecstasy of dance
have never fanned their inner flames to red hot life
i sing the truth of their sorrow and their sadness

i dance a waltz through the rooms of night
turn and swoop, swoop and turn til dawn
this coffee here, this sudden morning
i hold the world in my cup of earth

i search the east for the first gray of light
i settle down to see sun grow red like bellowed iron
its the radiance of birth that i crave

the spirit gives me the joy and splendor i crave
it crafts a covering of skin and veins for my soul
my body is spirit's robe and i wander in its heart
all this world's the mystery and my spirit is master

i am here to greet my father, the sun, at the river
i sing greetings to his gardens green, not yellow
this mother earth without water is dust and powder

sijo

sijo is a korean form which i am partial to. the first six
examples are a group choral music was written for by
frank j. oteri. the suite is called **(not) knowing the answer.**

(not) knowing the answer

(wait) (choose) (shout) (breathe) (move) (sit)

1 (wait)

wait in fear   wait in silence
empty self   empty nothing

answer back   reach conclusion
reach to toes   stretch in shouting

what one does   nothing matters
what one is   is all that is

2 (choose)

choose each time   to be a moment
choose each place   to be a where

choose a home   to be yours only
choose your heart   to be the door

widely open   to see sun's coming
wisely shut   this night so cold

3 (shout)

anger red   start and startle
peace is white   not heard, not heard

anger white   shout and bluster
blood is red   not seen, not seen

when we war   things are altered
when we kill   things are the same

4 (breathe)

seven stars   shine from nowhere
seven seas   wash the bottom

here we are   breathe in fresh air
grass is now   flounce of green hair

the funny thing   the funny laugh sense
wells from nothing   lives in nonsense

5 (move)

mist of morning   hot, dark coffee
feet on railing   bare, and carefree

constant foaming   constant movement
now is all things   now is all ways

hair is blowing   thoughts asunder
slow sweet breathing   air of wonder

6 (sit)

sit and wait   as a mountain
stand and shout   fast running gorge

scratch and till   make a garden
rain and sun   til thoughts grow large

sense is feeling   all is nature
sense is form   sense is sky

damp gusty cold   this march of wind
a biting mist   my future now

this face i ride   its warmth concealed
i grope my way   through blind eye's sight

no river ice   the boats all move
the waters move   the land stands still

murphy tired of a long cold winter

autumn sky   puffs cold magic
window's blue   cuts through this room

time so slow   has no meaning
now so now   stops heart in flow

this chair sits   holds to very being
this mind waits   sings its happiness

blue sky hidden   phantom sky
mist grey morning   when we die

tears are streaming   tears are lace
blue sky ridden   to this place

here is wish and feeling   here is wet
blue sky hidden   water's net

cool wind gusting   whipping tree
inside window   sipping tea

steam heat rising   blurry eye
tall thin shadow   hurry by

all is contentment   mist and air
a steaming body   new wet hair

don't bother with   a straw mat
we will sit on   fallen leaves

don't light   a pine torch
last night's   moon returns

let's drink   cloudy home brew
and nibble   salty pickles

eastern sun   fade westerly
water's flow   goes slow away

rising man   goes stumble man
dancing home   i'm river's fall

summer shadows   a dank cool wanting
summer shades   a long grey way

greying drops   of stained concrete
fuzzy steam   of black tar-ground

step in dream   miss the cut-glass
step in street   reach touching toe

stealing slowly   homeward steady
meeting this night   its city blows

late spring day   steal first feeling
this is all   sweet tomorrow

sniff the sun   strip and moisten
smell the heat   soak the sorrow

passing wings   calm warming senses
life begins   catches rising wind

look outside   cold clear window
look inside   gleam of mist

outside light   brings a warmness
inside light   fog of feelings

float away   this sense, this being
river sends   its waters down

pound on pound   goes my fist down
pound on pound   table scrape back

pound on wood   rattle bottles
pound full loud   fall back people

would my problems   scatter likewise
would my home   repel the rain

settle down   water run pool
carve a life   stone foundation

burst the dam   once, twice, three time
burst the heart   once, then no time

how the parting   brings the pain back
how the spring   brings back rapids

squeaking snow   beneath my feet
haloed moon   above my mind

opened coat   braving flurries
buttoned shirt   protected heart

careful steps   lead to open door
crackling fire   in welcoming eyes

summer green   yet a dreaming
winter chill   a choke cold hill

walk too far   shiver frost breath
walk too soon   suffer waiting

stretch to hear   a hidden message
stretch to see   round corner's bend

sun so pure   startle color
wind so warm   soon hurry spring

quiet gleam   wayward footstep
nascent green   still leading on

hurt is deep   still has no meaning
heart is earth   half buried stone

wander more   feet reluctant
wander there   beside the shore

river broad   sluggish dim brown
river wide   far windowed shore

sit to watch   the ceaseless moving
stand to feel   way home once more

war is come   dig through rubble
peace is gone   mist of tea time

strength is come   feeling gone now
numb is heart   smash all else down

why is sunshine   still here sometime
why is wind   so sweet in springtime

it's all there   each stab at perfection
each, tossed off   perceptive, witty, unique

one's own tone   an odd vernacular
one's own hand   scribble-scrabble meaning

one's own voice   formal, yet chatting away
one's own self   still and yet shares life

shih

```
bright    cool   wind    fresh      morning
walk      early  joy     rising     color
light     steps  ease    laughter   talk
time      now    always  here       now
```

bright walk light time
cool early steps now
wind joy ease always
fresh rising laughter here
morning color talk now

cold	sweep	bend	trees	limbs
lone	top	high	far	see
crisp	look	white	flow	cloud
blue	sky	mind	swim	down

cold lone crisp blue
sweep top look sky
bend high white mind
tree far flow swim
limbs see cloud down

early blossom heart stop beauty
smooth flesh   color first blush
soft   feel   crush hand touch
life   love   death   know loss

early smooth soft life
blossom flesh feel love
heart color crush death
stop first hand know
beauty blush touch loss

steam   hiss   bang   heat   rise
inside   noise   bang   cold   window
outside hear   rush   city   flurry
burst   mind   push   feel   snow

steam inside outside burst
hiss noise hear mind
bang bang rush push
heat cold city feel
rise window flurry snow

bramble creek tumble stone roll
sky bluster reddish leaves cling
mountain path fresh ready rain
sky water drench man robes

bramble sky mountain sky
creek bluster path water
tumble reddish first drench
stone leaves ready man
roil cling rain robes

            wang wei

man	leisure	apple	blossom	evening
quiet	night	spring	mountain	waiting
moon	rise	startle	mountain	bird
time	sing	now	middle	stream

man quiet moon time
leisure night rise sing
apple spring startle now
blossom mountain mountain middle
evening waiting bird stream

wang wei

haiku

slowly so slowly
i slip into fresh greenness
sloppy muddy ground

my heart sound echoes
in this fully leafed summer
soughing rustling breeze

heady crisp fall winds
straight from mountained horizon
eyes can see as far

the leaves are turning
much more the farther i go
cold creeps untoward

crimsoned vermont leaves
clinging to each maple tree
drops of waterfalls

paths in last stages
drying from a long day's rain
mind leafy collage

the days are numbered
each one shorter than the last
logs for the winter

to ease my passage
i welcome the black despair
middle of winter

mists slow sunny rise
this morning's looming mountains
colors grey subdue

rough exterior
soft center of nacrous self
being projects shells

the small huddled warmth
slumbers in kitchen corner
steam of morning's tea

cold stillness of top
through the bottom of deep well
mirror of my mind

quietness prevails
this long summer afternoon
occasional burp

does the flower grow
because of heat from the sun
or the bloom to be

twenty stories above
my feet are still wet marking
mud in early spring

longing for the wind
gathers dust as lung's sickness
gritty city smog

the pale yellow caves
peek through from closed draperies
the nights never sleep

snow gets in the way
of normal daily movement
but not words of love

brick orange sunrise
reflection of dying fire
in permanent camp

grass smells new mown blood
heaped away as browning green
smooth unbroken field

slow ease of winter
looses my inner jangles
to wear as jewels

   ,

true time compresses
through its various seasons
to train a tree small

shoveled snowy paths
guide sleepy circumspections
months before waking

the sun never shines
through that grimy barroom glass
but who looks outside

melting sooty snow
the first hint of city's spring
a hard crackling sleet

a rubaiyat

i am a lazy
i'm a contrary
i walk the hypotenuse
of square city streets

i look down the wind that always comes
here on this small land that's all we are
i watch the smoke of my fire go away
a slight smell remains at end of day

early morning arousal is immoderate
the light has yet to find harshness
the bed has not lost its pungence
we alone waking face the world

it's only a matter of integrity
to stand for polished thought
a non-tarnishing quicksilver
a sinewed ambiguity

i eat ice cream
i lick the spoon
i spoon hot songs
into my bones

the mind's differential
the sea of sins
i know
i can explain

to check a building
plumb to the sky
requires an insight
into cornerstones

xmas 67

purity is a wasted emotion
for giving is a human failing
the fact of force needs retelling
peace is an innovation

xmas 68

the ground is quiet, dormant.
an edge of snow stirs the air.
coldly, i stamp feet with care.
oh, would that the world gave warmth.

my love is like a nice cool night
it's shared with all the stars
it doesn`t seem that strong a bight
but strength is silken cords

the thin leafed trees are full with wind
a slow, soughing wind of coolness
i hear slip the moving night
the moon accepts its filling

i don't argue with my rhythm's surge
i bob on top and surf the wave
a swoop and curl, a flex and turn
then ease down slow into my cave

the magic carpet does not tempt my feet
i have no need for altitude nor vantage point
i dig my toes deep into the grass, the ground
the very substance i find all around

there is no music for the dance this special night
no practiced zeal to kick the bricks of pride
no fevered strum of rhythm's hues
just bustle of the sidewalk paying dues

when you sing your body tunes in habit
arches throat for a passion's peeling
holds the sound's expanded ceiling
regales the world with resounding space

i like it best when we don't talk
but grunt and thrash across the stage
in wrestle for the gristle on the bone
the plenitude of ordered older age

my animal lair is dense with my smell
it's dirty and small and it stinks
with nothing behind but hard scrabble down
i turn to face death glowing with pinks

my muse bustles around her piano bench
the nervous twitching starts in my left eye
i'm swamped in the gutter rhythm of her hips
so softly stroked as rhythmic sweep of sky

what's a library for if not to read
why keep a kitchen warm except to feed
i gather thoughts as i gather years
their boundedness my bounty clear

i don't eat like a lark
i eat with a spoon and fork
i don't kill freely with claws
i kill according to game laws

dive to the bottom of your river
risk the currents and the bends
wake your body to mortal terror
let your mind open to all earth sends

i learned long ago that the river knows
how and where to go down the spill
that water stored in mountain snows
reflects earth's breath, reflects earth's will

it's a cruel sad day in amarillo
with the wind from the north, and it's cold
the barbed wire fence holds out nothing
i'm as frail as this feather i hold

bend the future by remembering the past
inflate reality through acceptance
conflate the senses imaginatively
drown all due doubts in spring water

chappaqua, chippewa, who gives a shit
the wrap around or run around, she's gone
chapparal, cherokee, who stomps the dirt
the feathered hawk, or chicken scratch, it's me

i crowed to the sun when he appeared this morning
i rustled my wattles in a hullabaloo
this earth is mine to share for my time remaining
i'm here with you on our stomping grounds

i dig through piles and piles of thoughts
thrown into a box some long time ago
and wince in sum of exactness caught
in winking bug of soft dusk's glow

i got a brand new body just last week
i ordered it from the sear's catalogue
every twenty years or so i touch me up
a little nip, a little tuck, a little dye

i idle along my personal river
now grown fat and slow toward sea
wondering lazily when it will be
that sandy rip of deathly swirl

i know my enemy when i hold him in my hands
i feel his fear and anger, i dodge his thrust
i don't imagine that he has other aims
i hold to still, and then to kill

i love the mixing water of estuary
the crowded swirls of ecstasy
breathing fresh the gills of life
the resplendent health of blended edge

i need not know how hard it is
when i take the tumbling dive
that knifes through waters smooth
that flips a tail of gone, not here

i practice my music in the whole of its form
i can't stop the song and remember where
nor when nor how to keep on with the show
i start the strum and sustain the attack

i read a lot when i buy the books
i own them then, and have no teacher giving tests
no deadlines, themes, nor treatises
just thumbnailed pages special creased

i sit in the shade of a bank near ripples
the sun is dance of liquid fire
the glimpse of all i am comes fleeting
i hunker, still, there, there in my lair

i started as a boulder tumbling off the cliff
i smashed down the shoulder of the mountain
i made a creek for the earth's sweet tears
to run their course to the salty sea

i stretch the limousine which is my heart
i smooth a ground which oversteps the need
i park at end of the right side of street
i idle soft in luxury, i wait for love

i wander the keys of my life's piano
and pick around old memory's chords
my fingers twist in a wry abandon
making songs of my inner worlds

it's a matter of integrity
to stand for polished thought
a non-tarnishing quicksilver
of sinewed ambiguity

i've tossed my bait out into the pond
with floating cork to hold it off the bottom
i sit alert in a taoist watch
for the bobbing life in wisdom's pool

my backwardness becomes full forward
my ups have replaced all those young downs
my left has become my dominant eye
as hand of sword draws forth its words

my dampened dawn is grey with mist
the fire of youth banked to this steady now
another path lies before my feet
i wander slowly to meet day's grace

my daughters are sharing their first born child
the eldest handing daughter to backyard splash of aunt
i pound my stakes to straighten straggled garden
pour salt of sweat in eyes that tingle, tear

my ganglions have grown dull these last few years
they don't fire with the same force of raw ecstasy
they don't store with ease all the sounds i hear
they don't see with the keen eye of a child

my melody invites when out of tune
it jiggles jars of syruped yams
it winces childish suck on lime
it rankles hair on back of neck

my smell is concordant with fear
i stink of defeat and what it brings
where is the might of my sinew of youth
where goes the ground but under snow

my thoughts are creeks in their downward flow
thickening to pool and search cool depths
dropping in spray of rock's sharp spill
to final surge of tides in moon's salt rim

one should understand the balance of things
see joy in cold rain, in the fall visit spring in your mind
see the wisdom of age bought with a lifetime of effort
remember the lust for youth and its seductive glamor

the artist still knows why practice is all
you prosper alone when your order is set
when doing is love in its infinite get
and the quiver of fear brings beauty new born

the grass by my front door is dead and gone
worn down and killed by my daily pacing
you never come to see me, nor drink my tea
you've left me the always of expectation

the greens fresh picked are dark in leaf
and the water beads as oblate spheres
i grease the pan with light oil of life
and wilt with fresh bite of lemons

the kitchen i cook in has a warm, used look
the food i offer settles joy on the plate
brushes bowl of broth with taste
beckons with its bit of bacon

why are my thoughts always an ocean
not pond, or creek, or stream
but vast, unsettled and moody
not trickling or gouging earth's seams

why are you listening to all my ravings
why not dance alone to your own songs
you can't buy more than all your feeling
why sit at home when frogs know the moon

you yowl like a cat that feels the heat
you purr in a bass that murmurs its love
why should i ever not want you around
you tint my time with the gold dust of fairies

death song 41

sore comes the winter down
the implacable face of death
the cold bitterness within
the stubbornness of reality

when a circle becomes a community
when the string figure blossoms
an innerness of difference pertains
an intricacy of exact uniqueness

murphy holding with knowing hands